What Is Linguistics?

PRENTICE-HALL FOUNDATIONS OF MODERN LINGUISTICS SERIES

Sanford A. Schane

editor

John P. Kimball   The Formal Theory of Grammar

Sanford A. Schane   Generative Phonology

Maurice Gross   Mathematical Models in Linguistics

Suzette Haden Elgin   What Is Linguistics?

Other titles to be announced

What Is Linguistics?

SUZETTE HADEN ELGIN

University of California, San Diego
San Diego State University

PRENTICE-HALL, INC., ENGLEWOOD CLIFFS, NEW JERSEY

Library of Congress Cataloging in Publication Data

Elgin, Suzette Haden.
   What is linguistics?

   (Prentice-Hall foundations of modern linguistics series)
   Includes bibliographies.
   1. Generative grammar. 2. Linguistics. I. Title.
P151.E5   415   72-14103
ISBN 0-13-952408-8
ISBN 0-13-952390-1 (pbk.)

PRENTICE-HALL INTERNATIONAL INC., LONDON
PRENTICE-HALL OF AUSTRALIA PTY. LTD., SYDNEY
PRENTICE-HALL OF CANADA, LTD., TORONTO
PRENTICE-HALL OF INDIA PRIVATE LIMITED, NEW DELHI
PRENTICE-HALL OF JAPAN, INC., TOKYO

Editor's Note

Language permeates human interaction, culture, behavior, and thought. The *Foundations of Modern Linguistics Series* focuses on current research in the nature of language.

Linguistics as a discipline has undergone radical change within the last decade. Questions raised by today's linguists are not necessarily those asked previously by traditional grammarians or by structural linguists. Most of the available introductory texts on linguistics, having been published several years ago, cannot be expected to portray the colorful contemporary scene. Nor is there a recent book surveying the spectrum of modern linguistic research, probably because the field is still moving too fast, and no one author can hope to capture the diverse moods reflected in the various areas of linguistic inquiry. But it does not seem unreasonable now to ask individual specialists to provide a picture of how they view their own particular field of interest. With the *Foundations of Modern Linguistics Series* we will attempt to organize the kaleidoscopic present-day scene. Teachers in search of up-to-date materials can choose individual volumes of the series for courses in linguistics and in the nature of language.

If linguistics is no longer what it was ten years ago its relation to other disciplines has also changed. Language is peculiarly human and it is found deep inside the mind. Consequently, the problems of modern linguistics are equally of concern to anthropology, sociology, psychology, and philosopy. Linguistics has always had a close affiliation with literature and with foreign language learning. Developments in other areas have had their impact on linguistics. There are mathematical models of language and formalisms of its structure. Computers are being used to test grammars. Other sophisticated instrumentation has revolutionized research in phonetics. Advances in neurology have contributed to our understanding of language pathologies and to the development of language. This series is also intended, then, to acquaint other disciplines with the progress going on in linguistics.

Finally, we return to our first statement. Language permeates our lives. We sincerely hope that the *Foundations of Modern Linguistics Series* will be of interest to anyone wanting to know what language is and how it affects us.

Sanford A. Schane, *editor*

Note to the Teacher

This text is intended to serve as a general introduction to the field of linguistics for students with no previous background in the subject. The core of the discipline in terms of theoretical concepts and terminology is to be found in the first two chapters. The following schedule is suggested for a ten-week course:

Weeks 1 and 2	Chapter One
Weeks 3 and 4	Chapter Two
Week 5	Chapter Three
Week 6	Chapter Four
Week 7	Chapter Five
Week 8	Chapter Six
Week 9	Chapter Seven
Week 10	Chapters Eight and Nine

It is important that the student be thoroughly familiar with Chapters One and Two before going on to the rest of the book. Once those two chapters have been completed, the ordering of the other seven chapters is not crucial and may be changed at the teacher's discretion.

The readings suggested at the end of each chapter have been selected in order to refer students to other sources in each area of linguistics. The sources have been chosen for their generality and suitableness for beginning students. At the back of the book you will find a complete bibliography of all sources cited in the text.

If the text is used in a sixteen-weeks course at the junior college or college level, I suggest that it be supplemented by selections from the end-of-chapter bibliographies.

Any suggestions or criticisms that you may have as you use this book in your courses would be welcomed by the author.

Suzette Haden Elgin

Contents

Sociolinguistics   *69*

Stylistics   *81*

Applied Linguistics   *97*

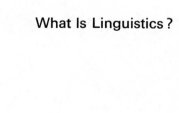

What Is Linguistics?

Introduction

In every known human society there are certain conversations which have become so fixed and so stereotyped as to have no real content beyond being the appropriate noises to make in specific social situations. The exchange that goes—"How are you?" "I'm fine—and you?" "Oh, fine, fine!"—is probably the classic example for English. Only rarely is the person who asks the question really concerned about the physical condition of the other, and even more rarely is any response but "fine" given, no matter how the person who answers may actually feel.

Another such situation, particularly in the United States, is where two persons who are total strangers suddenly find themselves face to face and obliged for politeness' sake to carry on the same sort of minimal conversational exchange. This occurs commonly enough at cocktail parties, faculty teas, business conventions, and the like, to have acquired its own set of ritual sounds and gestures, which go something like the following:

"I don't believe I know you. I'm Herman Jones." (Extended hand.)

"Glad to meet you. I'm Susan Brown." (Handshake.)

$$\text{"Are you a} \begin{Bmatrix} \text{professor?"} \\ \text{chemist?"} \\ \text{astrologer?"} \\ \text{Republican?"} \\ \text{nuclear physicist?"} \\ \text{radical?"} \end{Bmatrix}$$

$$\text{"Oh, no, I'm a} \begin{Bmatrix} \text{waitress."} \\ \text{student."} \\ \text{golf pro."} \\ \text{Unitarian."} \\ \text{dentist."} \end{Bmatrix}$$

All that is really meaningful in this exchange is the naming of the pair of professions or affiliations, which gives the two former strangers a basis, of sorts, for the next ten minutes of obligatory conversation. The ritual is satisfactory in most cases, and serves its purpose.

Let us suppose, however, that the persons addressed says, "Oh, no, I'm a linguist." Then what happens? The next line in this dialogue is usually just as predictable as the "How are you?—I'm fine" sequence. The response will be either:

"Oh, really? What's a linguist?"

or

"Oh, really? How many languages do you speak?"

Either remark comes as a shock to the linguist (at least the first half-dozen times), since he or she feels that the profession is not only important but probably the most interesting that can be imagined. Still it seems that the science of linguistics is as mysterious to most people (i.e., all nonlinguists) as, say Betelguesian hydro-electronics.

Unfortunately, someone who is genuinely interested in finding out what a linguist is and does will probably *not* be able to do so by asking a linguist. (Why this should be is yet another mystery.) To hear a linguist trying to explain his profession can be a painful, exhausting, and not very informative experience. Nor will it help a great deal to consult a dictionary, which will tell you that a linguist is "a person skilled in languages," or something similarly unhelpful.

If you were to visit the linguistics department of a university in order to discover what linguistics is by observing the people who study it, you would probably still come away puzzled. You would find classes arguing about such things as whether, in the sentence 'John almost forced Jennie to leave,' we can tell if Jennie left or not. You would find lengthy discussions going on about the difference in meaning between the phrases 'black bird's nest' and 'blackbird's nest', and how that difference is reflected in the sounds of the words. You would find students seriously struggling to determine what word our many-times-removed-great-grandparents might have used for 'bread'. These activities, interesting though they may be, will not give the observer a very clear idea about what makes up linguistics. Nor would it convey the reasons why those who dedicate themselves to the profession feel that linguistics is a fascinating and worthwhile field.

Because I am a linguist myself, and because my devotion to linguistics is a passion rather than a fondness, I hope that this book will clarify the mystery that independent investigation is likely to leave unsolved. Although written within the theoretical framework of generative transformational grammar, the book is not intended to make a trained linguist of anyone who reads it. Linguistics, like any other discipline, demands long years of arduous study and hard work. Instead, this book should serve as an introduction to more advanced and more specialized material, and should supply the answers to two specific questions:

1. What, exactly, is linguistics?

2. Why would anyone want to *do* linguistics?

In the event that this introductory book causes you to share the linguist's interest in the subject, you will find bibliographies at the end of each chapter that will direct you to sources of more detailed information.

Enjoy the book.

Phonology

All known human societies communicate by the method of meaningful sounds.[1] Human beings make many other, nonmeaningful sounds as well, however. For example, it is unlikely that a sneeze could ever be understood as having a meaning (other than the extralinguistic one that indicates physical discomfort). Still other human sounds may be meaningful in one situation but meaningless in others. Sounds like coughing, crying, throat-clearing, hand-clapping, and so on, may have meaning in specific contexts, but are very different from the sounds that actually make up human languages. Thus, although you may know when someone clears his throat loudly in the middle of a story you are telling, that there is some reason why you should not continue telling it, the throat-clearing sound is not the same thing as a meaningful word or series of words. Phonology concerns itself with the analysis and description of the *meaningful* sounds that human beings make.

Phonology has been with us for a very long time. All human beings are fascinated with the sounds of their own voices and with those sounds written

---

[1] The sign language of the deaf is of course an exception.

down. This fascination seems to have existed since the beginnings of recorded history. As early as the fourth century B.C. the Hindu grammarian Panini was writing about phonology; he was concerned to preserve the Vedic hymns absolutely unchanged, and this task demanded a meticulous description of the pronunciation of the words. Both Plato and Aristotle wrote works on language that contained phonological material. In China the scholar Shen Yao was writing about the tone system of the Chinese language around the fifth century A.D.

In this chapter we are going to discuss the basic concepts of phonology and take a brief look at the type of work being done by contemporary phonologists.

How Phonologists Characterize Human Speech Sounds

One of the important tasks of the phonologist is classifying the sounds of human speech. It is not enough just to say that a language has the sound *b* or the sound *r*, because there is no such thing as some one standard *b* or *r*. It is very important not to confuse letters—the alphabet of a language that is used to write it down—and actual speech sounds. If you have studied or if you speak either Spanish or French, you know that the sound represented by the letter 'r' is very different in both of those languages from that represented by 'r' in English. Phonologists need a clear method for describing just what they mean when they say that a particular sound is part of the sound system of human language. The symbols of the written alphabet of a language, its *orthography*, will not suffice to accomplish this task.

The traditional method for such classification has been in terms of two factors: first, the place where the sound is produced, and second, the way in which it is produced. These two factors are called the place and manner of *articulation*. In order to understand a classification on this basis it is necessary to examine the production of speech briefly in physiological terms.

The vocal organs, none of which has speech as its primary function, include the lungs, the windpipe, the larynx and pharynx, the nose, and the mouth. Within the larynx are the vocal cords. Within the mouth the tongue, lips, and teeth play an active part in speech production. The throat, nose, and mouth together are called the *vocal tract*. Figure A is a somewhat simplified side view of the vocal tract (see p. 6).

When a human being speaks, the air being exhaled from his lungs flows into the larynx, where the vocal cords are stretched across the air passage, and on out through the vocal tract. As he speaks, the vocal cords open and close very rapidly. (Phonologists have made films of the vocal cords and other areas of the vocal tract in action, so that linguists have been

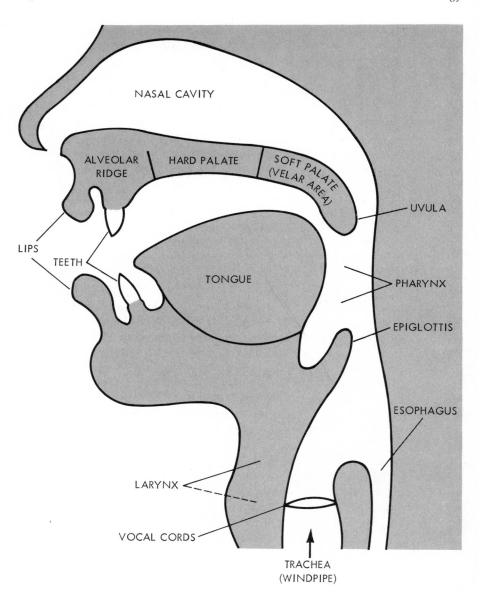

NASAL CAVITY

ALVEOLAR RIDGE

HARD PALATE

SOFT PALATE (VELAR AREA)

UVULA

LIPS

TEETH

TONGUE

PHARYNX

EPIGLOTTIS

ESOPHAGUS

LARYNX

VOCAL CORDS

TRACHEA (WINDPIPE)

FIGURE A

Note that the soft palate is lowered toward the back of the tongue, as in the production of a nasal sound.

TABLE I

ENGLISH CONSONANT SOUNDS CLASSIFIED BY
PLACE OF ARTICULATION

Labial	p, b, m, w
Labio-dental	f, v
Dental	θ, ð
Alveolar	t, d, s, z, l, r, n
Palatal	ch, j, sh, zh
Velar	k, g, ŋ
Glottal	h

NOTE: The symbol θ represents the sound of *th* in *thin;*
the symbol ð represents the sound of *th* in *bathe.*

able to study the actual mechanisms of vocal speech in detail.) The obstruction of this stream of air, together with changes in the shape of the mouth,
the closing off or opening of the nasal passages, and the movement of the
tongue in contact with the rest of the mouth are primarily responsible for the
sounds of human speech.

The consonant sounds of English have been classified in articulatory
terms as shown in Table I. *Labial* sounds, like *m*, have the lips as their
place of articulation; and if both lips are required to produce the sound, it is
called a *bilabial*. *Labio-dental* sounds require both the lips and the teeth
for their production. *Dental* sounds require that the tongue touch the teeth,
in this case the upper teeth. Behind the upper teeth lies the *alveolar ridge;*
alveolar sounds are produced by contact between the tongue and this bony
ridge. Moving back in the mouth, the tongue contacts the *palate*, and behind
that the *velar* area, to produce palatal and velar sounds. Finally, at the back
of the throat, *glottal* sounds are produced. Some phonologists divide these
categories even further, so that you will find terms such as *alveo-palatal*
in the phonological literature, but the classification shown in Table I is
adequate for the nonspecialist.

A good way to make the diagram clear is to pronounce each consonant
as you study the diagram and pay close attention to exactly where your
tongue touches other parts of your mouth, what part of the tongue is involved,
and so on.

A phonologist who wishes to discuss the difference between the sounds
of French and the sounds of English can use the sort of information in Table I
to present many useful facts. For example, the sound represented by the
letter *t* is an alveolar sound in English, but a dental sound in French. In
order to pronounce an English *t* the tongue must touch the alveolar ridge;
for the French *t*, however, the tongue touches the back of the upper teeth.

A classification of the consonants of English in terms of *manner* of articulation requires the explanation of a few technical terms.

In order to pronounce the English sound represented by the letter *b*, it is necessary to completely shut off the flow of air through the vocal tract. In fact, without a following vowel sound of some kind, a *b* cannot be made vocal. Such a sound is called a *stop*. The sound represented by 'b' in Spanish, when it occurs between two vowels, does not require this total blocking of the vocal tract; instead, air is allowed to escape with friction. This type of sound, which has a hissing or buzzing quality, is called a *fricative*. The English *b* and intervocalic Spanish *b* differ in that one is a stop and the other a fricative. Both are bilabial sounds.

In addition to stops and fricatives, English has *affricates*. An affricate begins like a stop but ends like a fricative. The affricates of English include the sound written as *ch* (as in *chair*), and if you listen carefully when you pronounce this sound you will hear that it begins like *t* and ends like the *sh* in *ship*. Notice that a language will not always use only one letter in its orthography to describe each speech sound. Both *sh* and *ch* in English represent single sounds, not sequences.

Nasal sounds are produced when the air passages of the mouth and nose are combined, not by blocking off the nasal passages as is often supposed. The nasal passage is opened by lowering the soft palate at the back of the throat which, in oral sounds, remains raised.

Liquids, the next sound category, require that the airflow be obstructed, but that air be allowed to escape by lowering one or both sides of the tongue.

TABLE II

ENGLISH CONSONANT SOUNDS CLASSIFIED BY
PLACE AND MANNER OF ARTICULATION

		Labial	Labio-dental	Dental	Alveolar	Palatal	Velar	Glottal
Stops	VL	p			t		k	
	VD	b			d		g	
Fricatives	VL		f	θ	s	sh		h
	VD		v	ð	x	zh		
Affricates	VL					ch		
	VD					j		
Nasals	VD	m			n		ŋ	
Liquids	VD				l, r			
Glides	VD	w				y		

And finally there are the *glides* (sometimes called the *semivowels*), which function like the consonants but require little more vocal-tract obstruction than do the true vowels.

In Table II the consonant sounds of English are classified in terms of both their place and manner of articulation. You will notice in looking at the chart that the sounds are also differentiated as *voiced* (VD) and *voiceless* (VL). A voiceless sound does not require that the vocal cords be vibrating during its production. In English both *p* and *b* represent bilabial stops, but they differ in that *p* is voiceless and *b* is voiced.

This articulatory way of classifying speech sounds is associated for the most part with the theory of *structural linguistics*.[2] Generative transformational theory is still interested in articulation but uses a slightly different method of classification, based upon a system of *distinctive features*.

Distinctive features were first proposed by a group of linguists known as the Prague school, and were further developed by the linguist Roman Jakobson. To understand just how a distinctive feature works, look at the table below, which classifies not sounds but a set of English names for animals.

	cow	bull	rooster
Female	+	−	−
Four-legged	+	+	−
Large	+	+	−
Domestic	+	+	+

Such a table is called a *feature matrix*. A feature matrix is prepared by choosing a set of particular characteristics that can be used to define the set of objects or entities to be classified, and then specifying each such object or entity as *plus* or *minus* that characteristic. Thus, the matrix above tells us that a cow and a bull are alike in that they share the characteristics of four-leggedness, large size, and domesticity, but unlike in that one is male and the other female. It tells us that the only characteristic, in terms of the matrix, that a rooster shares with a cow and bull is that it is also a domestic animal. You can see that the feature notation provides a simple and convenient method of description.

It will also be clear from examination of the matrix that if you have the feature [FEMALE] you do not need the feature [MALE], since [−FEMALE] will automatically provide you with it. This characteristic, that each feature has only the two values, plus or minus, is one of the most useful things about

[2] The methods of structural linguistics (also called *descriptive* linguistics) are primarily devoted to the classification of linguistic elements and the recognition of patterns within the classifications.

distinctive features. It is important to remember, however, that all features must express their value relative to some standard, and that the standard must be clearly defined. A rooster is small when compared to a bull, but quite large when compared to a mouse or a cricket.

A major problem for phonologists has been the choice of features and their adequate definition. In his book, *Introduction to Phonological Theory* (1968, p. 38), Robert Harms states this problem as follows:

> One goal is to obtain a single universal set of features, capable of adequately representing the phonological generalizations of all languages in a natural, direct manner. The basic set of features can be viewed as a hypothesis about language, subject to empirical validation.

The vocal tract of a native speaker of French does not differ from that of a speaker of Samoan, or Swahili, or Japanese, or any other language. Therefore, phonologists feel that a single set of features should be adequate to describe all human language.

In this book there will be no attempt to discuss the relative merits of the sets of features which have been proposed. However, Table III shows the stop consonants of English in terms of one proposed set, and is a representative example.

You will see at once that the set of English stop consonants does not really require all these features for its specification. No English stop can be a continuant, because the continuation of a stop is a physical impossibility. No English stop can be strident or nasal. These features, however, are needed to specify other consonants of English, and would appear on a complete English consonant feature matrix.

TABLE III

FEATURES OF ENGLISH STOP CONSONANTS

	p	t	k	b	d	g
Vocalic	—	—	—	—	—	—
Consonantal	+	+	+	+	+	+
Continuant	—	—	—	—	—	—
Strident	—	—	—	—	—	—
Nasal	—	—	—	—	—	—
Voiced	—	—	—	+	+	+
Anterior (front)	+	+	—	+	+	—
Coronal (articulated with front portion of tongue)	—	+	—	—	+	—

The distinctive features make it possible for a phonologist to uniquely define any of the sounds of English. For example, the sound represented by the English letter *p* can be defined as [+ CONSONANTAL], [− VOCALIC], [− NASAL], [− CONTINUANT], [− STRIDENT], [− VOICED], [+ ANTERIOR], and [− CORONAL].

Vowels, which are produced without obstruction of the flow of air through the vocal tract, can also be defined either in traditional articulatory terms or by distinctive features. English has both simple vowels like *i* in *pin*, and diphthongs, which are a vowel followed by an off-glide, like *ow* in *now*. (If you listen carefully as you pronounce *now*, you will see that there is a very slight *w* quality to the end of the vowel.) The relevant characteristics for describing English vowels are the following:

1. height of the tongue in the mouth [HIGH], [MID], [LOW]
2. location of the vowel at the front or back of the mouth [FRONT], [BACK]
3. rounding of the lips [ROUND]

The vowel *i* as in *machine* can thus be characterized as a vowel which is [+ FRONT], [+ HIGH], and [− ROUND]. The French sound represented by *u* in the word *rue* is also [+ FRONT] and [+ HIGH], but differs from the English vowel in that it is [+ ROUND] also. This is why it is useful for teachers of French to give students instructions like "say *i* as in *machine* and hold the sound, then round your lips" to help them learn to produce the French *u* in *rue*.

The problem of the relative nature of the distinctive features is more acute for the vowels than for the consonants. A consonant is either a stop or it isn't; there is no such thing as a partial stop, since the very definition of stop is the complete shutting off of the flow of air through the vocal tract. But describing a vowel is rather different. How high is a particular "high" vowel? How low is a "low" one? Some speakers may pronounce the vowel *o* as in *go* with almost no lip-rounding. This makes adequate characterization of vowels a little more difficult than similar characterization for consonants.

Not all of the distinctive features used by generative phonologists are based on articulatory information. For example, the feature [STRIDENT], which is part of the characterization of sounds like English *s* and *z*, is based on acoustic rather than articulatory information. On a spectrogram (a type of visual representation of speech sounds which will be discussed in more detail later in this chapter) strident sounds can be clearly distinguished from other sounds by their appearance alone. A [STRIDENT] sound produces large dark smudges on a spectrogram that are not produced by other sounds of English.

A phonologist does not classify the sounds of speech just "because they are there." If phonological research stopped at that point it would not be very interesting to study phonology. The phonologist goes on to make use of the information obtained from such classifications.

In the discussion that follows, the standard notation for sounds will be used. A symbol in italics, like *b*, represents the orthographical symbol used in writing a sound. A symbol which appears between slashes, like /b/, represents a phoneme. Finally, a symbol in brackets, like [b], is a phonetic symbol. The distinction between phonemic and phonetic will be made clear as the discussion progresses.

The Phoneme

A phoneme is a sound which the native speaker of a language knows to be a meaningful part of that language, and which enables him to make distinctions between words. For example, in English we have the two words *bill* and *pill*. These are different words with different meanings. The native speaker of English can distinguish between these two words in isolation only because of the difference between *b* and *p*. The same difference allows him to distinguish between *lab* and *lap*, or between *staple* and *stable*. English has many other pairs of words that differ in just this same way. For example, *pat/bat*, *pan/ban*, *pin/bin*, *cab/cap*, and so on.

A pair of words like those listed above, which differs only in one sound, is called a *minimal pair*. Because of minimal pairs like *bill/pill*, two of the phonemes of the English language, /b/ and /p/, can be isolated. By examining other types of minimal pairs, the phonologist is able to determine other English phonemes, such as /s/ (*sad/bad*), /v/ (*vile/bile*), and so on.

The English phoneme represented by the letter *l* is not always pro-nounced in the same way. Thus, if you say *leap* you will find that your tongue touches the roof of your mouth to produce the *l* farther forward than when you say the *l* of *bulk*. If a language had pairs of words that could be differen-tiated only by these two types of *l*, a native speaker would hear them as very different. However, there are no pairs of words in English that can be told apart only because of these two *l* sounds, and the English speaker hears them as the same. The phonologist is therefore able to say that there is a single English phoneme /l/, and that it has more than one pronunciation, depending on the context in which it occurs. The sort of difference exhibited by the two *l* sounds of English is called a *phonetic* difference (as contrasted with a phonemic one), and the different phonetic realizations of one phoneme are called *allophones*. The English phoneme /l/ has two allophones, but it is possible for a phoneme to have more than two.

The phonemes of a language each constitute a single sound segment for that language. These phonemes, as we have seen above, can be characterized in terms of their distinctive features. In addition, however, there are linguistic features which are not necessarily restricted to a single segment but may apply to several segments at a time. There are features which may be added to another phoneme. These features are referred to by various names, two of the most common being *suprasegmental features* and *prosodic features*, and they include such things as pitch, stress, tone, and the like. Compare the following:

(1)   a. *a blackbird's nest*
      b. *a black bird's nest*
      c. *a black birdsnest*

Phrase (1a) is the nest of a particular species of bird called a blackbird, (1b) refers to the nest of any bird which happens to be black in color, whether it is a blackbird or not; (1c) refers only to the color of the birdsnest itself.

Although these distinctions are made clear by the orthographic system of English, it is not the segmental phonemes like /b/ and /d/ and /s/ that enable an English-speaking person to tell the three phrases of example (1) apart when they are spoken rather than written. The segmental phonemes for all three sequences are absolutely identical. It is only the differences in stress and in juncture (separation between words) that allow us to distinguish these three sequences.[3]

In some languages the pitches of words can make a difference in their meaning. Such languages are called *tone languages*, and tone is said to be phonemic for such a language. For example, Navajo has a minimal pair which is differentiated only by tone:

azee⁽ˀ⁾   (low-toned, *medicine*)
azéé⁽ˀ⁾   (high-toned, *mouth*)

When a baby first begins exhibiting language, some time before he starts producing recognizable words, his babbling takes on the characteristic intonation of his native language, so that his parents often have the feeling that they *ought* to be able to understand what he is "saying." The suprasegmental features of the language are primarily responsible for this intonation pattern, and very often the failure to reproduce these suprasegmental features correctly causes an otherwise flawless pronunciation to be spotted immediately as a "foreign accent."

---

[3] It is juncture that allows a speaker to differentiate pairs like 'nitrate' and 'night rate'.

Acoustic Phonetics

In the discussion of the phoneme above, there was an occasional mention of phonetics, primarily articulatory phonetics. Articulatory phonetic distinctions have to do with such things as the degree of lip-rounding a given sound may have, whether a sound is followed by a burst of air (*aspirated*) or not, and how far forward in the mouth the tip of the tongue may touch in the production of some consonant. Differences between the speech of individuals are often described in these terms.

There is another branch of phonetics which concerns itself not with articulation but with acoustics, the physics of sound. The specialist in acoustic phonetics uses technical instruments that allow him to break down sounds for analysis in terms of their volume, pitch, duration, and similar factors.

One such instrument is the *sound spectrograph*. This machine converts the sound waves of speech into an electrical wave which can then be recorded on special paper to provide visible records of speech called *spectrograms*. Spectrograms show the vowels of the language as heavy dark bands, and the consonants as scattered marks, all indicated as occurring at specific frequencies.

Work with the spectrograph has provided linguists with much valuable information. For example, although phonemes are analyzed theoretically as single segments, examination of spectrograms show us that speech is really a

FIGURE B

Spectrogram of the word *alligator*. Phonetics Laboratory, University of California, San Diego.

continuum of sound. If you look carefully at the spectrogram in Figure B you will see that there are not empty spaces between each of the phonemes that would make it possible for us to say exactly where one sound ends and another begins.

The pitch of the speech of a five-year-old child is much higher than that of a forty-year old man, and the quality of their voices is very different. Nonetheless, we understand the word *cooky* when pronounced by the child and the word *cooky* when pronounced by the man as being one and the same word. The spectrogram makes it easier to understand this, since it shows us that even though the pitches of the sounds are different the basic *pattern* of any given word is the same no matter who pronounces it (provided the speaker does not have some actual abnormality of speech, of course).

This uniformity of speech patterns is due to the uniformity of human vocal equipment. It is true that the vocal organs of children are smaller than those of adults, but the relative size relationships among them are approximately the same.

Any doctor can tell you of having heard other doctors (usually older doctors with extensive experience) say that they can tell what is the matter with a patient from such "nonmedical" factors as the way he looks, the way he smells, and the sound of his voice. Recently a group of psychiatrists (Ostwald, 1965) has tested a portion of this claim by having made sound spectrograms of their patients' speech. They claim that not only is there a specific spectrographic pattern characteristic of normal voices, but there are also a number of such patterns which can be directly associated with specific psychiatric disorders such as schizophrenia and paranoia. If further research should bear out the accuracy of these claims, it is obvious that phonology will have provided the profession of psychiatry with a valuable diagnostic tool.

There are two applications of phonetics that would be very valuable to society. One is the construction of a machine which can take dictation from the human voice and print the result without the necessity for a human middleman; the extension of this development might allow the programming of computers by vocal input alone. The second is the development of a machine which would scan print and read it aloud, particularly for the use of the blind. Both the typewriter and the reader now exist in experimental prototype models.

The Task of the Phonologist

Every native speaker of a language is of course an expert on his own phonology, even though he may not be familiar with any of the linguistic concepts involved. Although he or she could not answer the question, "What are the phonemes of your language?" by providing the phonologist with a list, the native speaker knows at once when two words are a minimal pair, and which segment makes one member of that pair different from the other.

He also knows whether or not a particular combination of sounds is possible in his language. If an advertising man is trying to find a name for a new detergent (which means that he must find a new acceptable English sound sequence), he does not have to be a phonologist to avoid naming the product "Nguzz." He knows perfectly well that no English word can begin with the sequence *ng* and that no English speaker would be able to pronounce his product's name—sure death for the detergent. In addition, he would know that the sequence "Puzz" *would* be satisfactory because there could be such an English word and it violates no rules of English phonology.

This ability of the native speaker to determine what sounds mean something in his language and how they may or may not be combined into larger sequences is not something he must go to school to learn. It is simply part of the equipment that goes with being a native speaker.

This raises an interesting question. If every native speaker already has an internalized and perfect knowledge of the phonology of his language, what is there for a phonologist to do?

The answer is that the phonologist has only begun when he isolates the phonemes of a language and the rules for their combination. He must go on to provide as complete a description as possible of the entire sound system of the language with which he is working.

Part of this task is to discover the order that underlies what seems on the surface to be irregularity. Linguists know that no human speaker simply makes random noises, but rather that speech is governed by an orderly system of rules. When this system is obscured by its surface appearance, the phonologist uses his linguistic knowledge to explain the situation. He may show that what appear to be "irregular" verbs are not irregular at all, but are in fact quite predictable in terms of the phonological rules of the language. He may demonstrate that what appears to be a chaotic and indefensible spelling system—full of "silent" letters, for instance—is really a very sensible system in terms of the underlying structure.

Let's consider an example from English. The following set of English words contains one of these infamous letters, the "silent *g*":

(2) sign
     malign
     resign

An advocate of spelling reform might, if he considered only set (2), press for the elimination of this useless *g*, which seems to exist only to confuse the speller. But now look at another set of words:

(3)   signify
      malignant
      resignation

If we eliminate the "silent" letter from the words in (2), not only have we lost the relationship between the two sets of words, which was formerly obvious, but we will also find that English pronunciation rules will no longer allow us to say these words as we did before. For example, *sign* would become *sin*, and would then have to be pronounced like the same sequence in such words as *sinful*, *sinner*, and the like.

What these two sets in (2) and (3) tell the phonologist is the following: In the underlying structure of the words in (2) there really is a *g* sound, (the English phoneme /g/), eliminated later by the phonological rule of English that forbids a word ending in the consonant cluster *gn*. (If you try to pronounce the *g* in the words of (2) your own linguistic intuitions will tell you that such pronunciations would not be English.) Nonetheless, that the *g* is an actual part of these words at some deeper level of structure, before the application of the rule, is demonstrated by the fact that the *g is* pronounced whenever it occurs in an English word in a position which allows it to be pronounced, as in *signify*, *malignant*, and many others.

It is perhaps not very important to explain a few spelling examples from English. But what *is* important is that the phonologist can now point out that this is not just an isolated fact about the word *sign* at all. It is a general fact about the language, and the rule will apply every time a similar situation occurs.

This is not to say that the phonologist will always be able to explain every seeming irregularity. No one, not even a phonologist, could make the English verb *to go* regular, given the phonological shape of *went*. But in many cases the phonologists can show that under the surface chaos is hiding an underlying orderly system which, once understood, will make the correct production of forms a matter of course rather than of hazard.

Phonological Rules

The generative phonologist claims that the surface forms of sound sequences in a language are not necessarily the basic forms of those sequences. He claims that the *morphemes* of a language (the smallest meaningful units) have more abstract underlying structures which may change as the phonological rules of the language apply to them. We have already discussed one example, the English word *sign*, whose underlying structure contains the phoneme /g/, but whose surface structure has only /s/, /n/, and the diphthong /ay/.

The sequence of forms from the most abstract to the surface form is called a *derivation*. The surface form of a word or sequence corresponds to its actual spoken pronunciation. There are sequences to which few or no rules apply, and for which the deep structure will be almost identical to the surface structure. In other derivations a particular sequence may be subject to a number of different rules.

Phonological rules have various effects upon underlying segments and sequences. The rule that we have been discussing for the word *sign* removes a segment entirely and is called a *deletion* rule. Other rules may insert segments or simply change segments already there. Obviously, if a segment is deleted by the operation of a particular rule, nothing else can happen to that segment; similarly, for a rule to apply to a changed segment, that segment must have already undergone the rule that accomplishes the change. For this reason generative phonologists must place the rules of a language in their proper order to arrive at the correct surface structures.

The concept of rule-ordering can be made more clear by considering an example from English. English has two rules that effect changes in the English phoneme /t/ in particular situations. For example, /t/ becomes /s/ when it occurs immediately before a suffix beginning with the vowel /i/. This is the rule that changes the final /t/ of *pirate* to an /s/ in *piracy*. Another rule of English changes /t/ to /sh/ before *any* suffix-initial vowel. Thus, the /t/ of *delete* becomes /sh/ in *deletion*. Obviously, if this rule that changes /t/ to /sh/ applies *before* the other rule, the surface shape of *piracy* would have to be *pirashy*. Since no such form exists in English, phonologists know that the rule that changes /t/ to /s/ must apply first. These two rules are thus demonstrated to be ordered with respect to one another.

Generative phonologists use a standard notation (called a *formalism*) for writing rules. This formalism is far beyond the scope of this book. However, if we ignore for the moment the notation necessary to indicate that the vowel mentioned in the two rules above must be the first segment of a suffix, we can write the second rule as an example, as follows:

(4)   /t/ → /sh/   /_____V

This rule is to be read: "The phoneme /t/ is rewritten as /sh/ when it occurs immediately before a vowel." If this were a general rule of English, instead of a rule applying only to a suffix-initial vowel, English would never have any word containing a sequence of /t/ followed by a vowel.

The single slash in the rule in (4) is called an *environment bar*, the underscore indicates where the rewritten segment would occur, and the entire group of symbols to the right of the underscore (in this case, *V* for *vowel*) constitutes the *environment* for the application of the rule.

This rule could also be written in terms of distinctive features rather than phonemic segments. Extensive discussions of rule-writing and detailed derivations for morphemes are to be found in the phonological literature.

We have now surveyed in some detail the kinds of things that phonologists do in their work as linguists. We have seen that they are trying, among other things, to answer the following questions:

1. How are speech sounds produced by human beings?
2. How can speech sounds be characterized?
3. How can the difference between signals (like throat-clearing) and actual speech be characterized?
4. How are the sounds of speech combined to form sequences of sounds, and is this a systematic process or not?
5. Does regularity underlie the surface proliferation of "irregular" forms in languages?

A statement from Harms, *Introduction to Phonological Theory*, p. 12, makes a very appropriate ending for this chapter.

> The primary aims of generative phonology are to provide a phonemic representation of morphemes and a series of ordered rules that, together with information about boundary phenomena (junctures), (1) adequately express the phonological generalizations of the language and (2) at the same time determine the phonetic form of all utterances in the language.

SELECTED READINGS FOR CHAPTER ONE

GENERAL

DENES, PETER B., and ELLIOT N. PINSON. *The Speech Chain*. Bell Telephone Laboratories, Inc., 1963 (order from Garden State/Novo, Inc., 630 Ninth Avenue, New York 10036).

This book is a complete introduction to all aspects of human speech production—physiological, articulatory, and acoustic. It also includes some basic psycholinguistic sections on speech production. It is nontechnical, easy to understand, and intended for the layman. Highly recommended.

LADEFOGED, PETER. *Elements of Acoustic Phonetics*. Chicago: University of Chicago Press, 1962.

This book is an introduction to acoustic phonetics. It is somewhat more technical than *The Speech Chain*, but is intended for the beginning student and is not difficult to understand.

TRADITIONAL PHONOLOGY

GLEASON, H. A. *An Introduction to Descriptive Linguistics*. New York: Holt, Rinehart and Winston, Inc., 1955, 1961. Chapters 2–4, 16, 17.

This book is one of the classic texts of structural linguistics. The chapters recommended offer an ideal introduction to structuralist phonology for the beginning student.

HOCKETT, CHARLES F. *A Course in Modern Linguistics*. New York: The Macmillan Company, 1958. Chapters 2–13.

Slightly more complete, and a little more difficult, than Gleason. Moderately difficult for a beginner.

BLOCH, BERNARD. "A Set of Postulates for Phonemic Analysis." *Language* 24 (1948): 3–46.

HOCKETT, CHARLES F. "A System of Descriptive Phonology." *Language* 18 (1942): 3–21.

These two articles present the structuralist approach to phonology. Both are quite technical, and the beginner would do well to read one of the less complicated references before tackling these. Both are extremely clear and are considered landmark articles.

GENERATIVE TRANSFORMATIONAL PHONOLOGY

GRINDER, JOHN T., and SUZETTE HADEN ELGIN. *A Guide to Transformational Grammar*. New York: Holt, Rinehart and Winston, Inc., 1973. Chapter 11.

This chapter is a simple and nontechnical introduction to the theory and methods of generative transformational phonology. It is intended for the beginner.

HALLE, MORRIS. "Phonology in a Generative Grammar." In *The Structure of Language*, eds. Jerry A. Fodor and Jerrold J. Katz. Englewood Cliffs, N. J.: Prentice-Hall, Inc., 1964. Also in *Word*, 18 (1962): 54–72.

A brief article describing the generative approach, not difficult.

HARMS, ROBERT. *Introduction to Phonological Theory*. Englewood Cliffs, N. J.: Prentice-Hall, Inc., 1968.

This book is extremely technical and very complete. It describes many proposed feature systems, takes up the formalism of rule-writing, and provides extensive exericises (problems in phonology). It is of some difficulty for the beginner, but not impossible to work with. An excellent book.

SCHANE, SANFORD. *Generative Phonology*. Englewood Cliffs, N. J.: Prentice-Hall, Inc., 1973.

This book is the most complete introduction to generative phonology available. It is intended for the beginner and can be used by the student or reader with no background in phonology. Highly recommended.

Syntax

Good clear Introd.

Syntax is most easily defined as the rules for combining morphemes into larger units. When most of us think of our experience with grammar, it is the syntax that we remember—all those dreary days spent diagramming sentences and reciting the definitions of the parts of speech. Out of all those school years has come, presumably, a full knowledge on our part of the rules of our grammar, since that is what we were being taught.

But stop and think for a moment. Do you really know the rules of your grammar? Let's suppose a man walks up to you on the street and says he's doing a grammar survey. Do you know the rules of your grammar, he wants to know, and you assure him that you do; would you be willing to provide him with one of the more basic ones, he asks, and you assure him that you would. His question then is, "What is the rule for the formation of English questions?"

Would you be able to answer him? You should give very serious thought to this question, because your immediate reaction is likely to be that of course you could. You are basing that "of course" on the obvious fact that you are able to flawlessly *produce* English questions. But remember that you are also able to flawlessly produce the words of your language, and that this ability does not mean that you have conscious knowledge of the phonological rules behind what you are doing.

The rules of syntax, like the rules of phonology, are a part of your competence as a native speaker of English, and reflect the fact that you have internalized the entire grammar of your language. What the linguist wants to do, however, is to make that internalized grammar available not only to you as a native speaker but to anyone who might want to learn about your language. This means setting down the rules of the syntax in a form that anyone can understand and use. In this goal he is no different from the traditional grammarian who may or may not have called himself a linguist.

The word *competence* is a technical term in linguistics. It is used to describe that complete and presumably perfect knowledge of his native language that is part of the mental equipment of every native speaker. It is the native speaker's competence that allows him to produce the structures of his language, and in theory he should always produce them perfectly. In practice, of course, the speaker makes all sorts of mistakes and distortions; because although his *competence* is unlimited, the same cannot be said of his *performance* (also a technical term in linguistics). It is the speaker's competence that the linguist ordinarily wants to describe and not his performance, and you should keep this in mind when reading this chapter and in reading linguistic literature.

There is a basic difference between the goal of the traditional grammarian and the contemporary linguist. The linguist is not satisfied just to describe the *results* of how grammar rules work. He is not satisfied, either, with just any set of rules that covers the situation. His goal is to find the smallest, simplest, most economical set of rules possible for any given language: and that set must allow the native speaker to produce all the grammatical sentences of the language while it prevents him from producing any ungrammatical ones.

The ability of the native speaker to form sentences that he has never heard or seen before, and that may never have been used by anyone before, and to produce them on the basis of an internalized rule, is the source of the term *generative grammar*. Generative grammar (also known as *transformational* grammar[1]) is often assumed to have been invented, like a new household appliance, by Noam Chomsky of M.I.T. It is certainly true that the writings of Chomsky gave the contemporary school of generative grammarians their first impetus. However, Chomsky himself acknowledges his indebtedness not only to his teacher, Zelig Harris, but also to the French

---

[1] You will find these two terms used throughout linguistic literature as if they were completely interchangeable. This is not strictly accurate. A transformational grammar is only one possible type of generative grammar.

grammarians of Port-Royal and to a Spanish physician writing in the sixteenth century named Juan Huarte (Chomsky, 1968).

In his book *Language and Mind* (1968, p. 23), Chomsky gives a very clear and concise description of the goal of the linguist:

> The person who has acquired knowledge of a language has internalized a system of rules that relate sound and meaning in a particular way. The linguist constructing a grammar of a language is in effect proposing a hypothesis concerning this internalized system.

Now, remembering the difference between competence and performance, let's discuss how the linguist goes about discovering the rules of the native speaker's grammar.

Consider the following sentence of English:

(1)   *The student speaks the language.*

If you wanted to isolate the constituents of this sentence by dividing it into its major parts, where would you make the first break? Where is the largest and most obvious dividing point? As a native speaker of English, you know that it lies between *student* and *speaks*, as shown in (2):

(2)   *The student / speaks the language.*

Now take these two major chunks, one at a time, and apply the same procedure again. If you begin on the right, you get the division *speaks/the/ language*, and you can further break down the word *speaks* into its two morphemes, *speak/s*. You can go no farther with this portion; you have reduced it to its smallest meaningful constituents. The left side of the sentence will divide into *the/student*. You can now mark off all the constituents as follows:

(3)   *The / student / speak / s / the / language.*

You now have some idea about what the pieces of this sentence are. However, as a native speaker of English, you also know that there are some things very wrong with the schema used in (3) to illustrate these pieces and their relative positions. For instance, (3) would give us to believe that all of the marked-off units have an equal weighting in the sentence; that the word *the* has exactly the same grammatical status as the word *student*, and for that matter, that the *-s* in *speaks* has the same status as any of the words in the sentence.

Linguists are concerned with devising a means of setting down the constituent structure of languages in a way that will demonstrate just the sort of facts which we as native speakers know about our language and which make us aware of the inaccuracy of (3). A number of different systems (called *formalisms*) have been proposed. For example, Hockett (1958) has proposed a system usually called *immediate constituent analysis* which more clearly illustrates the relationships of the words in a sentence to one another. The following is a diagram of sentence (1) in the nested-boxes system he

The	student	speak	-s	the	language
				the language	
		speaks		the language	
the student		speaks		the language	
the student		speaks the language			
the student speaks the language					
The student speaks the language.					

proposed. This system for indicating constituent structure is far better than the simple marking-off of morphemes, as in (3). However, it still does not provide us with information on the roles played by the various constituents within the sentence.

Other systems which you will find in linguistic literature are *tagmemics*, associated primarily with Kenneth Pike, and the diagrams of *stratificational grammar*, associated primarily with Sydney Lamb. We will not discuss these systems here.

The system that will be presented in this chapter is that associated with transformational grammar. The transformational grammarian would take our English sentence and set it down as a *tree structure*, as in (4) below:

(4)

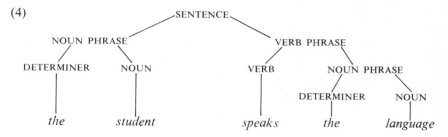

(Note that in this diagram the verb *speak* has already been combined with its third-person affix *-s*. This simplification will not affect the discussion which follows.)

In reading linguistic literature you will not find the tree structures in their full form as shown in (4). Instead, they are abbreviated slightly, and shown in the form of (5) below, in the interests of simplicity and economy of space.

(5)

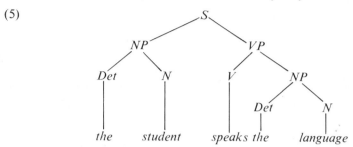

In examining tree diagrams you may find some items which are treated in a way you find unfamiliar. For example, you will often find a pronoun listed underneath the noun heading of a tree. This is just a matter of shorthand. The linguist knows that the members of the class of elements which can serve as subject of a sentence or as object of a verb include at least the following: proper noun, common noun, pronoun, and embedded sentence.[2] He uses the heading *N* or *NP* (usually referred to as the *node N* or *NP*) to indicate a member of this class. A fully detailed tree would, of course, specify the differences among these members.

Phrase Structure Grammar

From the examination of a tree structure like that shown in (4) and (5), we can tell a number of things about the syntactic organization of the English language. For example, we can tell that the two most basic units of the English sentence are the Noun Phrase and the Verb Phrase. The linguist writes this information in a shorthand form known as a Phrase Structure rule, as in (6).

(6)   *S → NP VP*   (A sentence is rewritten as a Noun Phrase followed by a Verb Phrase.)

Another thing that examination of the tree will tell us is that the proper order of a determiner relative to a noun in English is *before* it, and that one

---

[2] The sentence 'I know that Bill is sick' results from the *embedding* of 'Bill is sick' in the upper sentence.

possible way of constructing an English *NP* is to place a determiner before a noun. This will give us another rule, as in (7):

(7)   *NP → Det N*

We can tell, also, that within a verb phrase the direct object *NP* must follow the verb in English, and that one possible rule for the formation of an English *VP* is the following:

(8)   *VP → V NP*

The linguist now has three Phrase Structure rules which recapitulate the structure shown by tree (5), as follows:

(9)   a.   *S → NP VP*

b.   *NP → Det N*

c.   *VP → V NP*

This is a small and economical set of rules. It can be used to generate thousands of grammatical sentences of English; for example, all of the following:

(10)   a. *The girl sings the madrigals.*

b. *The elephants destroyed the plantation.*

c. *A Spaniard saw the Frenchman.*

d. *An animal ate the grass.*

You will recall, however, that the set of PS rules must be capable of generating *all* the possible grammatical sentences of the language. Obviously, our set of three will not accomplish this task. Our grammar is not even adequate to handle the following very simple sentences:

(11)   a. *John speaks Swahili.*

b. *John speaks terrible Swahili.*

c. *The tall student tripped.*

The linguist must now do something about his set of rules to allow him to generate this last group of sentences as well as the others. Take the first one, 'John speaks Swahili'. This is very like the sentence with which we began this discussion, 'the student speaks the language', except for one important difference—there are no determiners present in the sentence.

The rule is easily modified by using the linguistic convention which says that elements in a rule, when enclosed in parentheses, are optional. The rule would then read as follows:

(12) $NP \rightarrow (Det) N$

That is, an English *NP* may or may not contain a determiner.

In order to take care of (11b) and part of (11c), we need only indicate the optionality of another element, as follows:

(13) $NP \rightarrow (Det) (Adj) N$

This will take care of 'tall student' and 'terrible Swahili', both of which are *NP*s containing an adjective. It will also let us know that the following structures cannot be generated by the grammar of English:

(14) a. * *tall the boy*

     b. * *boy the tall*

     c. * *boy tall the*

(It is customary in syntax to indicate ungrammatical structures by an asterisk in this fashion.)

We now have left only the *VP* portion of 'the tall student tripped', and by this time the linguist's next move will be obvious to you. He simply encloses in parentheses the *NP* listed in the Verb Phrase rule, to show that not all English verbs must be followed by an *NP*. Now we have a set of three rules again, but they are modified as follows:

(15) a. $S \rightarrow NP\ VP$

     b. $NP \rightarrow (Det) (Adj) N$

     c. $VP \rightarrow V (NP)$

This set of rules, which is very small and very limited, is called a Phase Structure Grammar (PSG). You will notice that it doesn't have any prepositional phrases in it as yet, or any adverbs, or any conjunctions. It is obviously inadequate. Nonetheless, in order to see what the linguist does, we will remain with this small PSG, which is adequate to generate many (but not all) English sentences.

Look very carefully now at (15a) and see what it actually tells us. It says, in effect, "Every English sentence must have a noun phrase and a verb phrase, and the noun phrase must precede." This sounds reassuringly like the familiar rule about subjects and predicates, except for the remark about ordering, and should come as no shock to anyone. But is the rule correct? Can it be said, absolutely and without question, that every English sentence must contain an *NP* and a *VP* or it is not grammatical? The answer is "no." Consider the following sentence, which is certainly grammatical:

(16) *Jump!*

There is no *NP* in this sentence Our rules will not generate it, yet we know it to be a good English sentence. And it is precisely at this point that the linguist brings in three very important terms: *deep structure*, *surface structure*, and *transformation*.

Deep Structure, Surface Structure, and Transformation

You may remember that in school you were taught that the subject of a sentence like (16) was a curious item called an "understood *you*." The linguist agrees with the principle being expressed here, but feels that it can be put in a more useful way. The fact that every native speaker of English feels intuitively that (16) does have a subject *NP*, although it isn't there before his eyes, bears out the fact that the rule *S → NP VP* is correct. The linguist wants to maintain this rule. If it can possibly be avoided, he does not want to have to say that there are two kinds of English sentence, one containing an *NP* subject and one without. Not only would such a statement complicate the grammar, it would ignore the fact that every speaker of English "understands" a subject to be present in the second type of sentence.

Instead, the transformational grammarian takes the position that the *deep structure* of the sentence 'Jump!' does contain an *NP*, like any other English sentence, and looks something like the following:

(17)

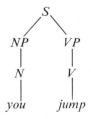

In order to get from this deep structure to the surface structure 'Jump!', what is needed is not an additional PS rule, but rather a *transformational*

rule. This transformation will delete the *NP* 'you' which has been generated by the PSG. It is called *Imperative Deletion*. It is not a PS rule; it takes the result, the output, of a PS rule, and operates upon that output to give us another output, the surface structure.

motivation

One of the major parts of any transformational linguist's work is showing evidence for the proposals that he makes. This is called *motivating* a proposal. In the case of the *Imperative Deletion* transformation above, we have seen no motivation for the rule as yet. The fact that the hypothesis of a 'you' in deep structure is in accord with the native speaker's intuitions is fine, but it does not constitute evidence in the linguistic sense.

There is evidence for this deep structure 'you', however. Look at the following sentences.

(18)   a.   *I wash myself.*

      b.   *We wash ourselves.*

      c.   *He washes himself.*

      d.   * *I wash yourself.*

      e.   * *We wash myself.*

      f.   * *He washes herself.*

As you can see, the only way a grammatical sentence of this type can occur is for the deep structure to contain a subject *NP* and an object *NP* that refer to the same individual. Such a pair of *NP*s is called a *coreferential* pair, and their coreference is indicated in tree structures and sentences by a small subscript *i*. The deep structure of (18a) would be the following:

(19)

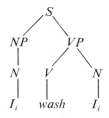

A transformational rule called the *Reflexive* rule will then apply to this deep structure and will replace the second 'I' by the reflexive pronoun 'myself'. The first 'I' in (19) is called the *antecedent*.

Now, consider once again the pattern shown by the imperative sentence. There is a grammatical sentence of English, 'Wash yourself'. Since the reflexive pronoun 'yourself' can only result from a deep structure in which there was a coreferential pronoun 'you' as its antecedent, we know that the deep structure of 'Wash yourself' must have had 'you' as its subject. This constitutes linguistic evidence for the presence of the deep structure subject 'you' in imperatives.

The reflexive evidence also tells us something about the ordering of the two rules *Reflexive* and *Imperative Deletion*. It tells us that the *Reflexive* rule must be ordered before the *Imperative Deletion* rule. If this were not the case, the subject 'you' would be deleted by *Imperative Deletion* and would no longer be there to serve as antecedent for the *Reflexive* transformation. The result would be the ungrammatical sentence in (20):

(20) **Wash you.*

There is another transformation of English which depends upon a pair of coreferential noun phrases. This is the transformation called *Equi-NP Deletion*. Consider the following sentence:

(21) *Patricia wants to leave.*

Sentence (21) is the result of a lower sentence, 'Patricia leave(s)' being embedded in a higher sentence, 'Patricia wants (something)'. The deep structure looks like the following:

(22)

```
                    S
          _____/ _____
        NP                   VP
         |              ____/  \____
         N             V           NP
         |             |            |
     Patricia_i      wants          S
                            _____/ _____
                          NP               VP
                           |                |
                           N                V
                           |                |
                       Patricia_i         leave
```

The rules of English syntax forbid a surface structure like the deep structure of (22). That is, there can be no English sentence 'Patricia$_i$ wants Patricia$_i$ to leave'. (That is not to say that such a sentence never can occur; an adult might use such a sentence to a child, or it might occur as a joke or in some other special circumstance. But in normal speech it is not a grammatical sentence.)

There are of course many sentences like the following:

(23) *Patricia wants Benjamin to leave.*

But this sentence is the result of a deep structure in which the two *NP*s are not identical, as in (24).

(24)

```
                        S
              _____/ _____
            NP                    VP
            |               ____/  \____
            N              V            NP
            |              |             |
        Patricia         wants           S
                                    ___/  \___
                                  NP         VP
                                  |           |
                                  N           V
                                  |           |
                              Benjamin      leave
```

In this case the conditions for applications of *Equi-NP Deletion* are not met, and therefore the second *NP* remains.

Some transformations of English are considered to be optional. For example, the rule that produces 'Yesterday there was a riot' rather than 'There was a riot yesterday' is entirely optional. The *Reflexive* transformation and *Equi-NP Deletion*, however, are not optional but obligatory. Just as there are no sentences like 'Bill wants Bill to leave', where 'Bill' and 'Bill' refer to the same individual, there are no sentences of the form 'He is washing he' or 'He is washing him' where the two pronouns are coreferential.

The linguist constructing a grammar, therefore, first attempts to identify the meaningful constituents of the language. He puts together a set of Phrase Structure rules from the facts he learns about their possible combinations. Then he determines what transformations are necessary in order to derive all possible surface structures from the resulting deep structures.

Every human being who is a native speaker of a language is walking around with just such a grammar in his head, complete in every detail. No linguist has yet succeeded in achieving the same perfection and completeness, but that is the goal toward which he works.

Universal Grammar

It would enormously simplify the linguist's work if all languages had the same syntax, and the differences were only to be found in the lexical items (a common misconception of beginning foreign language students). If you consider closely related languages, it often appears at first as if this might be a workable idea. For example:

(25) a. *John speaks French.*

    b. *Pierre parle anglais.*

    c. *Maria habla español.*

These three sentences from English, French, and Spanish, can all be generated by the PS rules $S \rightarrow NP\ VP$ and $VP \rightarrow V\ NP$. Since these languages are closely related historically, it is not surprising to find that they share some rules in common. However, consider the following set:

(26) a. *He speaks French.*

    b. *Il parle anglais.*

    c. *Habla español.*

Here, even in these simple sequences, the word-for-word surface correspondence of structure with only the phonological shape of the words differing breaks down. If we move to more complex sentences, the situation becomes even worse, as in (27):

(27) a. *He doesn't speak French.*

    b. *Il ne parle pas anglais.*

    c. *No habla español.*

When a linguist uses the term "universal grammar" he is not referring to such correspondences as those shown in (25). What he refers to, instead, is those universal *properties* that are to be found in every human language. Two of these are, of course, the processes of negation and interrogation. No human language lacks these two properties, and linguists feel that the ability to comprehend both is a part of the innate equipment of the human brain. (This is discussed in more detail in Chapter Five.) It is hard to imagine how a parent might go about explaining to a child what asking a question *meant*, if the child's mind was literally empty of that concept.

The linguist is interested in determining the complete set of properties which characterize the syntax of human language, and then in explicitly stating the ways different languages lexicalize (express in words) those properties.

One of the most essential properties of human language is *recursion*. Because of recursion there can be no such thing—in terms of competence— as a longest possible sentence. Consider the following:

(28) a. *Angela is a very beautiful woman.*

  b. *Angela is a very, very beautiful woman.*

  c. *Angela is a very, very, very beautiful woman.*

As you can see, we could go on indefinitely adding new instances of *very* to (28a), as if at that point there were a loop in the sentence that we could follow as many times as we liked.

  Sentences like (28c) are of course not very common in everyday speech, although they are perfectly possible. Another type of sentence that shows recursion is perhaps more common. Consider the following:

(29) *Jack says that Mary is beautiful.*

To this sentence we can now add a potentially infinite number of additional embedded sentences, as shown in (30):

(30) a. *Jack says that Mary is beautiful.*

  b. *Jack says that Bill knows that Mary is beautiful.*

  c. *Jack says that Bill knows that Martha thinks that Mary is beautiful.*

  d. *Jack says that Bill knows that Martha thinks that Phil agrees that Mary is beautiful.*

Not even →

In performance terms, of course, there *is* a longest sentence, because the human speaker would eventually collapse with exhaustion or lose his voice. But in theory you could always add one more embedded sentence, one more instance of *very*, or simply say *and* and go on with additional lexical material.

  No human language lacks the property of recursion. It is part of universal grammar and thus part of the definition of what constitutes a human language.

  The specialist in syntax cannot take anything for granted when he considers the *surface* manifestations of grammatical properties. Each time he says to himself, "There could not be a language that did not have a . . . " he is in for trouble. For example, the Eskimo language appears to have no first-person pronoun. Some languages have a plural, others manage quite well without. The idea of "noun" and "verb" varies widely from language to language. In the midst of all this diversity, in surface terms, another quotation from Chomsky (Language and Mind, p. 76) seems appropriate.

> It is reasonable to suppose that a generative grammar is a system of many hundreds of rules of several different types, organized in accordance with certain fixed principles of ordering and applicability and containing a certain fixed substructure, which, along with the general principles of organization, is common to all language.

The linguist working in syntax studies new languages, as well as the more familiar ones, in order to add ever more data to the information we now have about languages as a whole. It is his hope that this will enable us one day to make clear statements about the content of universal grammar and thus to specify exactly what conditions must be met for some group of vocalizations to be considered a human language; he also hopes to specify what must be the basic language equipment of a newborn human being.

Generative Semantics

In early transformational theory, as developed by Chomsky, there was a basic assumption that the grammar was separated into three individual *components*. These were referred to as the phonological component, the syntactic component, and the semantic component. Chomsky claimed that there could be no mixing of these three levels of grammar. Thus no syntactic information could be used in phonology, no phonological information in syntax, and so on.

More recently, linguists have begun to question this rigid separation of grammar levels. As a result, generative transformational grammar has split into two theoretical camps—those who still insist upon separation of levels, the Extended Standard Theorists, and those who feel that this position cannot be maintained, the Generative Semantics advocates. In this introductory book it would be inappropriate to go into the arguments for each of these two positions. However, some of their basic theoretical assumptions can be briefly summarized here.

Generative Semanticists claim that the deep structure must contain all the information necessary for the meaning of the sentence, and that the syntactic structure and the semantic structure are one and the same. Thus, a deep structure tree is assumed to contain all the information relevant to meaning, from whatever source. Extended Standard Theorists, on the other hand, propose surface rules of semantic interpretation to handle phenomena that would otherwise seem to require a mixing of levels. The Extended Standard Theory is associated primarily with Chomsky; among the more prominent Generative Semanticists are George Lakoff and James McCawley.

The theory of generative transformational grammar is a rapidly developing one, and many new and exciting changes can be expected to take place in the next few years. The professional journals of linguistics, for example *Language*, *Linguistic Inquiry*, and *Lingua*, are probably the best sources for the student who wishes to keep abreast of these new developments.

SELECTED READINGS FOR CHAPTER TWO

TRADITIONAL SYNTAX

GLEASON, HENRY A. *An Introduction to Descriptive Linguistics*. New York: Holt, Rinehart and Winston, Inc., 1961. Chapters 10 and 11.

This is an excellent, easy-to-follow introduction to the methods of syntactic analysis in structuralism.

SAPIR, EDWARD. *Language*. New York: Harcourt, Brace and World, Inc., 1921, 1949. Chapters 4 and 5.

A simple, nontechnical discussion of traditional syntactic analysis, with examples from a number of languages.

TRANSITIONAL

HARRIS, ZELLIG. "Co-occurrence and Transformation in Linguistic Structure." In *The Structure of Language*, eds. Jerry A. Fodor and Jerrold J. Katz. Englewood Cliffs, N.J.: Prentice-Hall, Inc., 1964, pp. 155–210.

This is a landmark article and presents the type of pretransformational grammar to which Chomsky has himself acknowledged his indebtedness.

GENERATIVE TRANSFORMATIONAL SYNTAX

CHOMSKY, NOAM. *Syntactic Structures*. The Hague: Mouton, 1957.

Chomsky first presented his linguistic theory in this book, which is probably the most familiar to the nonspecialist. It is very clear, but is definitely not for the beginner with no linguistic background.

————. *Language and Mind*. New York: Harcourt Brace Jovanovich, Inc., 1968.

This brief book is a good general summary of Chomsky's theory. It is not difficult and serves as an excellent introduction to more advanced transformational materials.

JACOBS, RODERICK A. and PETER S. ROSENBAUM. *Transformations, Style and Meaning*. Waltham, Mass.: Xerox College Publishing, 1971.

The simplest possible introduction to transformational theory and transformations. It presupposes no linguistic background and is highly recommended.

LYONS, JOHN. *Introduction to Theoretical Linguistics*. Cambridge: Cambridge University Press, 1969. Chapter 6.

This is a more advanced presentation and is somewhat technical, but very clear. It deals with such topics as Phrase Structure grammars and rule-writing, as well as the more basic concepts. In addition, in the chapter cited and others, Lyons discusses some of the competing systems of grammar theory. Not an easy book, but one of the most complete. Highly recommended.

Semantics

It is very common to hear someone involved in an argument with another person say something like, "But that's just semantics!" The very frequency of such remarks would seem to indicate that we all know what semantics is, and certainly the request for a definition of semantics will almost always be met with a ready reply—"Semantics is *meaning*." That's all very well, and a matter of general agreement. But the agreement stops short at the next question: "What is meaning?"

A description of all the attempts at defining what is meant by "meaning" would require the space of this entire chapter. It would have to include Bloomfield's claim that a form's meaning is "the situation in which the speaker utters it and the response which it calls forth in the hearer," a definition that in effect includes the entire universe of discourse. It would have to include traditional definitions in philosophical terms. It would have to include the more recent attempts to define meaning in terms of sets of semantic features. And still, at the end of the chapter, no real agreement on what "meaning" means would have been reached.

Therefore, in this chapter we will arbitrarily set aside the problem of a formal definition of meaning and assume that the field of semantics has such a definition, even if it cannot be precisely formulated.

If it is simply taken for granted that the meaning of a word is a matter known (very roughly) to all native speakers of a given language who are familiar with that word, we can move on to other problems.

Remember that in generative transformational theory, grammars are said to have at least the following three components: the phonological, the syntactic, and the semantic. We will ignore for the moment the question of the separateness of these components, and attempt to answer two questions:

1. What would a semantic component have to be able to do?

2. How is the operation of the semantic component to be represented in the grammar?

The Task of the Semantic Component

One of the tasks of the semantic component would be to account for relationships that exist among sets of linguistic forms. The first such relationship is *paraphrase*—that is, the semantic component must be able to account for the fact that native speakers consider some sequences of language to be synonymous with others.

The following pair of English sentences is considered to be synonymous:

(1)   a. *Hermione put the football down.*

   b. *Hermione put down the football.*

The exact limits of this paraphrase relation are not easy to specify. It is clear that sentences that are one hundred percent synonymous are going to be rare. For example, is the following pair synonymous?

(2)   a. *My brother is a vegetarian.*

   b. *My brother does not eat meat.*

Certainly these two *could* be synonymous, but it is simple to devise contexts where they would not be. If 'my brother' does not eat meat just because he dislikes the taste of the stuff, sentence (2b) is true of him but sentence (2a) is not. Therefore, we cannot say that the sentences of (2), in isolation, are synonymous.

The problem with (2), of course, lies in the definition of the lexical item 'vegetarian', and is not difficult to describe. More difficult is the problem of deciding whether the two sentences of (3) are synonymous.

(3)   a. *John ate the spaghetti.*

      b. *The spaghetti was eaten by John.*

There is no problem of definition in (3). The meanings of the terms 'John' and 'spaghetti' remain constant in the two sentences. What is true of (3a) is true of (3b), and vice versa. And yet many native speakers of English feel that there is some subtle difference between these two sentences. One common statement about the difference is that (3a) is about John, but (3b) is about the spaghetti. A semantic component would have to specify this difference and make clear why the two sentences of (3) are or are not synonymous.

A second relationship that the semantic component must account for is *contradiction*. The two sentences of (4) are contradictory.

(4)   a. *Alec has been devoured by a bear.*

      b. *Alec has not been devoured by a bear.*

The relation of contradiction may also lie in the definitions of single lexical items, as in (5).

(5)   a. *Hilda is remarkably fat.*

      b. *Hilda is remarkably thin.*

A semantic component would have to make all this specific.

Now there are difficulties about the precise determination of the relations of paraphrase and contradiction; however, both concepts are easily grasped by speakers.

The third concept that a semantic component would have to deal with is not so clear-cut. This is the problem of *ambiguity*. Speaker judgments about ambiguity are not so immediate and straightforward as those about paraphrase and contradiction.

A sequence of language is said to be ambiguous if it has more than one possible *semantic reading* (that is, more than one meaning). The following sentence is one of the classic examples of ambiguity:

(6)   *Flying planes can be dangerous.*

This sentence can be paraphrased by either of the sentences below:

(7)   a. *It can be dangerous to fly planes.*

      b. *Planes that are flying can be dangerous.*

The two sentences of (7) would have very different deep structures, and nothing about the surface structure of (6) in isolation will allow a speaker to determine which of the two deep structures it corresponds to.

Interestingly, speakers do not always realize that ambiguities exist in sentences. For instance:

(8)   *They are cooking apples.*

Anyone reading this sentence may not be aware of any possible ambiguity. However, once the ambiguity is pointed out to him, he will not only recognize it but be able to provide further examples of the same kind. This ability is part of his linguistic competence.

Sentence (8) can be paraphrased by either of the following:

(9)   a. *They are apples for cooking.*

      b. *What they are doing is cooking apples.*

(Of course, sentence (8) is not ambiguous if spoken, because the stress patterns are different for the two possible meanings. Thus, the semantic reading of (9a) is 'They are *cooking* apples', while (9b) requires 'They are cooking *apples*'.)

A semantic component must be able, then, to account for the relationships among various linguistic structures such as paraphrase, contradiction, and ambiguity.

In addition, a semantic component would have to match every structure generated by a grammar with its associated meaning or meanings. Thus, given a sequence like /bɪl#ɪz#ɪn#ðə#triy/ (the # symbol indicates a word boundary), and the tree structure to which it corresponded, the semantic component would have to be able to match both of these, or their combination, with the meaning the native speaker of English associates with the surface structure 'Bill is in the tree'. It is not at all clear just how this would be accomplished.

There is not as yet any really adequate description of a semantic component. One of the most complete attempts at providing such a description is that of Jerry Fodor and Jerrold Katz (1964). In the Fodor and Katz theory, it was proposed that the semantic component must consist of a dictionary of the lexical items of a language (called a *lexicon*), and a set of rules (called *projection rules*) that would provide semantic interpretations for sentences. The dictionary entries would contain phonological markers to specify the pronunciation of a lexical item, syntactic markers to specify its part of speech and the various syntactic functions it might fill, and semantic markers to specify its meaning.

The set of semantic markers for a language would contain items like
[± HUMAN], [± MALE], and so on. In addition, there were special markers
called *distinguishers* to indicate contexts for lexical items, in order to make it
possible to account for an ambiguous lexical item. Thus, the lexical item
'plane' can refer either to a carpentry tool, a means of transportation, a
geometric term, or an abstract metaphorical extension of that geometric
term, as in: 'His conversation was on an entirely different plane than it had
been the previous day'. The distinguishers would indicate which of these
contexts the item was associated with for any deep structure containing the
lexical item 'plane'.

The projection rules of the semantic component would operate upon a
tree, to which the lexical items and all the information from the lexicon
would be attached, and by working up that tree would provide a semantic
interpretation.

Notice that this system does not mention any information outside that
provided by the components of the grammar itself. There is no appeal to
extralinguistic information. Is it possible for the semantic component to
accomplish its task in this way? One example from English will suffice to
show that it cannot. Consider the sentences in (10), (11), and (12).

(10) a. *Mary asked me to dance, but I didn't dance.*

      b. *Mary asked me to dance, but I didn't.*

(11) a. *Mary asked me to leave, but I didn't leave.*

      b. *Mary asked me to leave, but I didn't.*

(12) a. **Mary asked me to come to her party, but I didn't come.*

      b. *Mary asked me to come to her party, but I didn't.*

      c. *Mary asked me to come to her party, but I didn't go.*

You can see that in (10) and (11) a verb is being deleted from the (a) sentences,
under the condition of identity with another verb present in the sentence, to
produce the (b) sentences. In (12), however, although there is a (c) sentence
corresponding to the other (b) sentences, the two verbs involved are not
identical. What is going on here?

It seems clear that although at the level of deep structure the two verbs
of (12) may be roughly identical, at the point where a choice must be made of
a lexical item to insert at the bottom of the deep structure tree, it is not
possible to select an identical one. Notice that the following pair is perfectly
all right, and conforms to the pattern of (10) and (11):

(13) a. *Mary asked me to go to her party, but I didn't go.*

      b. *Mary asked me to go to her party, but I didn't.*

Charles Fillmore has pointed out that the difficulty here lies in the orientation of the speaker of a sentence using the verbs *come* and *go* to factors in the outside world. Consider the following examples:

(14) a. *I will come to your office tomorrow.*

   b. *I will go to your office tomorrow.*

Fillmore has noted that sentence (a) can only be used if the speaker assumes that the person he is speaking to will be present at the office in question when he arrives there. The (b) sentence, on the other hand, makes no such assumption.

There does not seem to be any way to devise a semantic component that would be completely self-contained and still account for such factors as those that determine the choice of *come* and *go* in English. There may be other such verb pairs as well. For example, in this writer's dialect the two verbs *bring* and *take* show the same pattern, as in (15).

(15) a. *She asked me to bring her books to her, but I didn't.*

   b. *She asked me to bring her books to her, but I didn't take them.*

   c. *She asked me to bring her books to her, but I didn't bring them.*

The study of semantics is at this point one of the most exciting and fast-developing fields of linguistics. Much progress is being made, not only for English, but in the semantics of other languages as well.

Linguists must arrive at a really satisfactory definition of "meaning." They must account for the way in which the sound sequences of any language are paired with their meanings by the grammar. They must decide if the semantic component can be kept rigidly separate from the rest of the grammar, and if it can operate without extralinguistic information. If extralinguistic information must be available to the semantic component, as the evidence seems to indicate, then linguists must determine how this is to be incorporated in the grammar. The work of accomplishing all these goals should provide absorbing material for study in the years ahead.

SELECTED READINGS FOR CHAPTER THREE

TRADITIONAL SEMANTICS

BRÉAL, MICHEL. *Semantics: Studies in the Science of Meaning.* New York: Dover Publications, Inc., 1964.

   This is one of the classic descriptions of traditional semantics. Of moderate difficulty.

LYONS, JOHN. *Introduction to Theoretical Linguistics.* Cambridge: Cambridge University Press, 1968. Chapters 9 and 10.

In these two brief chapters Lyons covers all of the major concepts of traditional semantics. The description is very thorough, very clear, and not at all difficult. Highly recommended.

ULLMANN, STEPHEN. "Semantic Universals." In *Universals of Language*, ed. Joseph H. Greenberg. Cambridge, Mass.: M.I.T., 1966, pp. 217–55.

This is a nontechnical article on many aspects of semantics, with examples from a number of languages.

TRANSFORMATIONAL SEMANTICS

GRINDER, JOHN T., and SUZETTE HADEN ELGIN. *A Guide to Transformational Grammar*. New York: Holt, Rinehart and Winston, Inc., 1973. Chapter 7.

This is a complete treatment of the Katz and Fodor model for semantics. It is intended for the beginner and is easy to understand.

KATZ, JERROLD J., and JERRY A. FODOR. "The Structure of a Semantic Theory." In *The Structure of Language*, eds. Fodor and Katz. Englewood Cliffs, N. J.: Prentice-Hall, Inc., 1964.

This is the landmark article in transformational semantics. It is of moderate difficulty.

KAY, MARTIN. "From Semantics to Syntax." In *Progress in Linguistics*, eds. Manfred Bierwisch and Karl Erich Heidolph. The Hague: Mouton, 1970, pp. 114–26.

A brief article on current semantic theory. It is somewhat technical, but not difficult.

Historical Linguistics

When we think of history we are accustomed to think of successions of kings, of sequences of wars, of conquests and discoveries, of one political system giving way to another. All these share a common characteristic, at least when we consider the events of the past thousand years or so. This characteristic is a matter of precision, of facts that we can locate exactly in time in a neat linear succession. Thus we know, when we talk of American history, that the Pilgrims landed at Plymouth in 1620, that the Emancipation Proclamation which declared all the slaves to be free was issued on January 1 in the year 1863, and so on. Even if we go much farther back in history—for example, to ancient Egypt or Mesopotamia—we are still able to give reasonable dates for many events, and we know which event followed another.

When we come to the history of human language,[1] however, the situation is markedly different. We cannot point to any particular date when language began, nor do we know what was the first language of mankind.

---

[1] The study of language at a given point in time, usually contemporary, is called *synchronic* linguistics. The study of the changes and developments of a language through time is called *diachronic* linguistics.

Our written records of languages date back only a little more than a few thousand years. How many years before that writing may have begun, we do not know. In view of this situation, just what does the historical linguist hope to do? How does he work, and upon what sort of foundation can he make his claims?

To answer this question we must first make clear a few basic matters about which there is often confusion. The most important is probably the meaning of the much-abused word "primitive." We are continually tripping over this word in historical studies, in all fields. We read of "primitive man" and "primitive society," of "primitive architecture" and "primitive tools." We find certain tribes living today described as having a "primitive life."

In a very general way we can be certain that the use of "primitive" in such expressions as "primitive man" is equivalent to "prehistoric man"— that is, to a stage previous to any written records upon which to base conclusions. When contemporary peoples are described as primitive, however, the word is not given the same meaning except by analogical extension. When the natives of the Kalahari are said to be living a "primitive life," what is meant is that technologically, and in material terms, these people live in a manner more consistent with what we assume to be true of prehistoric man's life than with our own.

Because of this terminological fuzziness, there has been a general tendency to assume that primitive peoples—in either sense—have primitive languages. Now, when we speak of a primitive dwelling as compared with a contemporary one, we can be pretty sure of what we mean. We mean a mud hut or a cave or a shelter of sticks as compared with our own homes. But what about a primitive language? Can we point to some language and say, "This is what a primitive language is like"?

We cannot. No group of human beings today, no matter how their lifestyle may appear to us, speaks anything that could be called a primitive language. No records have ever been found of anything that could be called a primitive language. The most ancient languages for which we have written texts—Sanskrit, for example—are often far more intricate and complicated in their grammatical forms than many contemporary languages.

A truly primitive language would be inadequate for ordinary human communication. For example, such a language might have no mechanism for adding a new word when a new object was introduced into the culture speaking it. No such language exists.

The second general question has to do with the idea of a "first" human language. Although linguists feel certain that at some remote period in prehistory there was a single language that was the ancestor of all languages spoken today, we do not know what that language might have been, or when it began, or where it was spoken. Many theories have been proposed, but all remain just that—theories.

The historical linguist, then, finds himself in much the same situation as the paleontologist. The paleontologist takes scraps of evidence—a bone here, a fossil there—and by combining these scraps with the principles of the scientific method by which he works, he proceeds to tell us about the appearance and habits of prehistoric animals. This process is called *re-construction*. When you go to a museum and see exhibits of dinosaurs rampant with smaller animals in their mouths, you are not looking at an exhibit prepared from written records and pictures, but at a reconstruction.

The historical linguist is the paleontologist of language. From a few surviving clues, and the extrapolation of the principles of historical linguistics, he attempts to reconstruct languages that have now disappeared. He must take up the history of language in midstream, after written records of it already exist, even though he knows that the appearance of writing must be a very late stage in the development of language. That he can do this at all is due to what we know about the process of language change over time.

Language Families
and the Comparative Method

There are around four thousand languages spoken in the world today. (The number varies according to how strictly one defines the terms "language" and "dialect.") Linguists divide these languages into families and subfamilies of related languages—related because they can be assumed to have shared a common ancestor. Table I on p. 46 lists the major language families of the world, with a few members of each family as examples. Note that there are some languages that do not seem to have any relatives at all, such as Basque, and others with relatives all over the world, like Indo-European.

All these human languages, and the thousands of others not listed here, are assumed by linguists to have developed from one common ancestral language. There are two major theories about this development. The first, called the *family tree* hypothesis, assumes a development as shown in (1) below.

(1)

TABLE I

LANGUAGE FAMILIES OF THE WORLD*

1. INDO-EUROPEAN

    A. Germanic (English, Dutch, Swedish)
    B. Celtic (Breton, Irish, Welsh)
    C. Romance (French, Spanish, Roumanian, Portugese)
    D. Slavic (Russian, Polish, Czech, Bulgarian)
    E. Baltic (Lithuanian, Latvian)
    F. Iranian (Persian, Kurdish, Afghan)
    G. Indic (Hindi, Urdu, Punjabi, Sinhalese)
    H. Albanian (Albanian)
    I. Armenian (Armenian)
    J. Greek (Modern Greek)
    K. Tocharian (extinct)
    L. Hittite (extinct)

2. FINNO-UGRIC (Finnish, Estonian, Hungarian, Lappish)

3. ALTAIC

    A. Turkic (Turkish, Azerbaijani, Uzbek)
    B. Mongol (Mongolian)
    C. Manchu (Manchu)

4. BASQUE (Basque)

5. AFRO-ASIATIC

    A. Semitic (Hebrew, Arabic, Amharic, Ethiopic)
    B. Egyptian (Coptic)
    C. Berber (Kabyle, Zenaga)
    D. Cushitic (Somali, Galla)
    E. Chad (Hausa)

* The examples given are by no means all-inclusive.

6. NIGER-CONGO

    A. West Atlantic (Bulom, Fulari)
    B. Mande (Kpelle, Bambara)
    C. Kwa (Akan, Yoruba, Ibo)
    D. Gur (Mussi)
    E. Central (Efik, Tiv, and the Bantu languages such as Swahili
       and Zulu)

7. JAPANESE (Japanese, Korean)

8. SINO-TIBETAN

    A. Tibeto-Burman (Tibetan, Burmese, Garo)
    B. Chinese

9. KADAI (Thai, Laotian, Shan)

10. MALAYO-POLYNESIAN

    A. Indonesian (Malay, Javanese, Tagalog, Malagasy)
    B. Eastern (Hawaiian, Samoan, Fijian)

11. AUSTRALIAN (Walbiri)

12. DRAVIDIAN (Tamil, Gondi)

13. AUSTRO-ASIATIC (Khasi, Santali, Khmer, Vietnamese)

14. AMERICAN INDIAN

A. Algonquian	H. Mosan
B. Natchez-Muskogean	I. Penutian
C. Iroquoian	J. Hokan
D. Siouan	K. Mayan
E. Caddoan	L. Uto-Aztecan
F. Tunican	M. Athabaskan
G. Eskimo-Aleut	

Tree (1) shows that some language, Language A, has split into two languages, B and C, and that Language C has subsequently split into languages D and E. Languages B, C, D, and E are all said to be related because they had Language A as their common ancestor. Languages B and C are said to be *daughter* languages with respect to Language A, and *sister* languages with respect to one another.

The second hypothesis about language development through history is called the *wave* hypothesis. It assumes that languages spread out from a central source like waves, rather than neatly splitting off as they do in (1).

Actually, these two theories are not incompatible. As Robert A. Hall has said (1950), "the 'family tree' is a schematic description of the *occurrence* of changes; the 'wave theory' covers the description of their *spread*."

All linguists agree that the family tree idea cannot be an accurate statement of actual language development; people do not go to bed one night using one language form and get up the next morning using another. On the other hand, the idea that language change occurs in tiny increments resulting in gradual change over a long period of time is not accurate either. We will return later in this chapter to this question of just how languages change.

It is likely to come as something of a surprise to a speaker of English to find that his language is a member of the same family as Bulgarian and Hindi. It is easier for him to see the relationship between English and German, because the shared history of these two languages is comparatively recent and the surface resemblances are still striking. The following table shows parallel forms from four contemporary Germanic languages:

ENGLISH	SWEDISH	DUTCH	GERMAN
blood	blod	bloed	Blut
hand	hand	hand	Hand
father	fader	vader	Vater
sister	syster	zuster	Schwester
hail	hagel	hagel	Hagel
hut	hydda	hut	Hütte
death	död	dood	Tod
birch	björk	berk	Birke
wind	vind	wind	Wind
door	dörr	deur	Tür

Because all of these languages are living languages, we can be certain of the pronunciation of each of these forms. We know, for example, that although the English word *wind* is spelled exactly like the German one, the German word is pronounced as though it were spelled with an initial *v*. If this table dealt with languages no longer spoken (Ancient Greek or Latin, for example), we would be able to point out only the correspondence of orthographical units, not sound units.[2]

It does not take a trained linguist to come to the conclusion that the four languages above are all related. Granted, then, that they shared some common ancestor language, what does the linguist know about that ancestor from such data as provided by parallel forms?

If you examine the table closely, you will be able to see not just shared letters, but shared *patterns* of letters, and this is what is important to the linguist. The inventory of possible human phonemes is rather small, with most languages having somewhere between thirty and forty members of that inventory represented. Hawaiian is at one extreme with only eleven, and at the other are Caucasian languages with about seventy. Almost every known language has an *a* sound, an *o* sound, and at least one nasal. In view of all this, the simple fact that two languages both have some of the same sounds means very little. What matters is the systematic shared patterning of sounds, far beyond the possibility of coincidence.

The linguist examining the table will see a number of patterns almost at once. For example, all four languages have a two-syllable form beginning with an *s* or *z*, having a *t* at the beginning of the second syllable, and ending with an *r*. All four of these forms refer to the same meaning—a female sibling. The odds against four languages showing a phonological pattern like this, and all four forms having the same meaning, are astronomical unless we assume a family relationship. We see four words, all referring to the liquid which flows in human veins; all four begin with *b* and end with *d* or *t*. It is this sort of correspondence that the linguist looks for, and such word sets are called *cognate sets*.

If the linguist wished to set up an inventory of the phonemes of the Germanic ancestor of these four languages, he could almost at once set up a phoneme /b/, since all four languages show total agreement about this. The phoneme would then appear in his work as /*b/, since reconstructed phonemes are by convention marked with an asterisk. In the future you might think of the dinosaurs at the Smithsonian as being branded with an invisible asterisk.

It takes many sets of related forms to establish and support a historical relationship. This is because it is not difficult to find a pseudocognate or two

---

[2] We are not entirely without information on this point, however. We have grammatical descriptions written by ancient scholars. We have information gathered from the observation of systematic spelling errors. In some cases we can learn much about the pronunciation of dead languages by studying the rules of their poetry. For example, when we find the two words 'bind' and 'wind' used as rhymes in English poetry during a period when the rules for rhyming were very strict, we know that they must have been pronounced alike at that time. We can apply the same type of analysis to the poetry of languages that are no longer spoken.

from almost any pair of languages. For example, Modern Greek has a word *mati* and Malay has a word *mata*; both words mean 'eye'. We see here a possible pattern correspondence, a two-syllable word beginning with *m*, having a *t* in the middle, ending with a vowel, and sharing the same meaning. In order to establish some relationship between Malay and Modern Greek, however, we would have to discover many such sets, all showing a correspondence between Greek *m* and Malay *m*, between Greek *t* and Malay *t*, and having Malay *a* where Greek has *i*. This is not possible, and we are therefore safe in attributing the pair of words for 'eye' to chance alone.

Correspondences like this between unrelated languages are usually due to one of two factors. They may be due to coincidence, as in the example given above. They may also be the result of both languages having borrowed a single word from another language, or one language having borrowed a word from another. The Navajo have a word *gidi* which means 'cat' and is pronounced almost exactly like 'kitty'. From this we do not postulate a relationship between English and Navajo, but rather recognize *gidi* as a loanword. French has *le weekend* and *le whiskey*, both borrowed unchanged from English even though they radically violate the rules of French orthography. Amazingly enough, English has borrowed from French the expression *chaise longue*—literally 'long chair'—and retained the French spelling but insists upon pronouncing the words as if they were written 'chase lounge'.

When a language borrows a word from one of its sister languages *after* the split between them has occurred, as is the case for *gestalt*, for example, that word is not the result of their common linguistic heritage but is as truly a loanword as if it had come from some totally unrelated language. Sometimes a language will have both a related form and a borrowed form, each of which can be traced to a common ancestor.

The linguist who attempts to demonstrate a historical relationship has to be very careful about such things as word-borrowing, since he must not confuse loanwords and cognates, and it is very easy to do so.

Now let's reconsider the process we have been describing. As you can see, it consists of finding sets of forms that share a common meaning, that show a systematic common patterning of sounds, and that are too numerous to be the result of chance or borrowing alone. This technique is called the *comparative method*.

The reconstruction of Indo-European has been the proving ground for the comparative method, because linguists are fortunate enough to have access to many ancient written texts for these languages. It had its "official" beginnings in 1786, when a scholar named Sir William Jones presented an address establishing the historical relationship of Sanskrit to Latin, Greek, and the Germanic languages, thus making it possible to have Indo-European texts dating back to at least as long ago as the fourth century B.C.

The fact that the working principles of the comparative method have been borne out and reinforced by the available written records for Indo-European languages has made it possible for linguists to apply these same methods, with confidence, to language families for which no written records exist, or for which writing is a very recent development.

Phonological Reconstruction

One approach to the comparative method of reconstruction was the claim that there are *no* exceptions to sound change. This means that you cannot ever make a rule that sound *X* in one language corresponds to sound *Y* in some other language, and then follow it with a list of forms to which the rule does not apply. This position was a very strong one, and was particularly associated with a group of linguists called *neogrammarians*. It now seems clear that it is too strong, and that there are other factors to be considered besides the single rule in question—for example, there may be two or more rules competing at the same time.

But the basic concept behind this idea—that sound change is regular and systematic—is correct. One of the most famous examples bearing this out is the "law" of Jakob Grimm for the problem of consonant shifts in the Germanic languages. Grimm's Law stated that Indo-European aspirated stops corresponded to unaspirated stops in Germanic, that Indo-European voiced stops corresponded to Germanic voiceless stops, and that Indo-European voiceless stops corresponded to Germanic fricatives. Grimm based his law upon comparative examination of many sets of forms from older Indo-European languages like Greek and Sanskrit with forms from the Germanic languages. For example, Greek *podos* is the ancestor of English *foot*; Sanskrit *nábhas* is the ancestor of German *Nebel* (fog).

The fact that there were many sets of Germanic forms that did not seem to conform to Grimm's Law was enough of an annoyance to set many linguists working to account for these apparent exceptions.

One troublesome set of exceptions was not in the Germanic forms but in the Sanskrit. Gothic (a Germanic language) had a word for daughter, *dauhtar*. Sanskrit had a word that was obviously related—*duhitá*. However, since Germanic voiced stops were supposed to correspond to Sanskrit voiced aspirated stops, the Sanskrit form should have been *dhuhitá*, which it obviously was not. Similarly, Gothic *biudan* ('offer') should have had as a cognate Sanskrit form *bhodhāmi*, but in fact this Sanskrit word began not with an aspirated *b* but with *b* alone, *bodhāmi*.

In order to solve this problem, the linguist Grassmann resorted to *internal reconstruction* instead of the comparative method. In internal reconstruction the linguist must rely on information from within the single language he is working with. Grassmann knew that in Sanskrit the past perfect tense (as in 'I have eaten') was marked in a characteristic way. The first consonant of the verb root would be repeated, a process called *re-duplication*, and followed by a vowel. Thus, from the present tense for 'give' (*dō*) Sanskrit formed the past perfect *dadau*. Every past perfect form therefore should have included two identical consonants separated by vowels in this same fashion.

But the Sanskrit form for 'he has become' is *babhūva* instead of the expected *bhabhuva*, and there are many, many similar pairs. How was this to be explained?

Grassmann saw that the explanation for the seeming irregularities in the Sanskrit perfect tense also explained the apparent exceptions to Grimm's Law. He noticed that the only time a consonant was not reduplicated in the Sanskrit perfect was when the second consonant in the form was aspirated. He therefore proposed that there was a rule of Sanskrit forbidding two aspirated consonants in successive syllables of a single word. Thus, when the present tense of 'become', which began with *bh*, reduplicated to form the perfect, the original '*bh*' became unaspirated to conform to this rule. By the same rule, the Sanskrit word for daughter could not possibly be *dhuhitā* because it would have contained two successive aspirated consonants. Grassmann was able to show that the irregularity was not in the Germanic consonant shift itself, but rather internal to Sanskrit.

Generative phonologists would say that the underlying form of Sanskrit 'daughter' is indeed *dhuhitā* and that there is a surface phonological rule of Sanskrit that changes the initial *dh* to *d* to produce the surface form *duhitā*. The neogrammarians did not describe the facts in these terms, but were concerned with explaining the surface forms in order to eliminate the forbidden exceptions.

When a historical linguist works with a language like Basque, for which there are no related forms whatsoever because there are no known related languages, he must rely entirely upon internal reconstruction. In most cases, however, linguists use both techniques in combination, choosing the most appropriate one for the problem at hand, and checking the results of each method against the results of the other. In this way he works "up" the tree toward the earliest forms of the language that can be reconstructed, called *proto-forms*. Such proto-forms make up the *proto-language*. Thus, when a linguist talks of Proto-Indo-European, he is referring to the earliest stage of Indo-European that linguistic techniques will allow us to reconstruct.

Morphological and Syntactic
Reconstruction

All of the historical changes we have discussed so far have concerned the phonology of languages. Much historical work has also been done, and is being done today, with the *morphology* of languages—i.e., such things as the morphemes that indicate the tense of verbs, the gender of nouns, whether words are singular or plural, and the like. You will remember that morphemes may be full-scale words like *house* and *remembrance* and *inability* and *the*, or they may be meaningful portions of words such as the letter *s* in the English plural, or the suffix *-ing* in *singing*.

When a linguist works with the history of a language, some of his most useful material is likely to be found in the history of morphemes, particularly with regard to the various affixes of words. This work with the *morphology* of a language often turns up additional evidence for historical relationships.

The morphology of the English language has changed radically over time. English was once a very highly inflected language with many prefixes and endings. For example, the following table represents the Old English forms of our third-person pronouns:

	he	she	it	they
Nominative (*Subject NP*)	hē	hēo	hit	hīe
Accusative (*Direct Object NP*)	hine	hīe	hit	hīe
Dative (*Indirect Object NP*)	him	hiere	him	him
Genitive (*Possessive NP*)	his	hiere	his	hiera

Not only the pronouns, but also the nouns of English once had declensions of the type we associate with Latin and Greek. The declension for the noun *day* in Old English was the following:

	Singular	Plural
Nominative (*Subject NP*)	daeg	dagas
Accusative (*Direct Object NP*)	daeg	dagas
Dative (*Indirect Object NP*)	daege	dagum
Genitive (*Possessive NP*)	daeges	daga

English has changed from a language with many complex inflections, as shown in the tables above, to one with almost no inflections at all. All that is left are the plural markers, the *s* that marks the third-person singular present tense, the *-ed* of the past tense, the *-ing* of the present participle, and the comparative and superlative endings *-er* and *-est*.

In syntax, too, we find changes. English today forms yes/no questions by requiring the use of a certain kind of verb called a *modal* verb. By inverting a modal verb and its subject we produce questions like the following:

(1)   a. *He can sing. Can he sing?*

       b. *He may leave. May he leave?*

       c. *She will scream. Will she scream?*

When a sentence does not already contain a modal verb, the rules of English grammar require the insertion of the modal 'to do', as in the following examples:

(2)   a. *He sings. Does he sing?*

       b. *She screams. Does she scream?*

There was an earlier stage of English, however, when all questions of the yes/no type were formed by simply inverting the subject and verb. This was not so long ago; the following examples are taken from Shakespeare's *King Lear*:

(3)   a. *"But goes thy heart with this?"*

       b. *"What say you to the lady?"*

       c. *"Why brand they us with base?"*

       d. *"Think you so?"*

Most historical work to date has been confined to phonology and morphology, but more and more work is now being done in historical syntax.

Language Change: The Generative Transformational Approach

You will remember that at the beginning of this chapter the two theories of historical change—the family tree hypothesis and the wave hypothesis— were discussed in some detail. Both these traditional approaches focus on the language itself, as if language change were like geological change. It was easy for linguists who were concentrating upon sets of linguistic objects (words) to forget that the whole point of language is that it is one of the defining characteristics of a human being. Language is spoken by people, and it does not change of itself but through the speech of people. Paul Kiparsky (1968, p. 342) has stated the feeling of generative linguists toward such change as follows:

> The point is simply that a language is not some gradually and imperceptibly changing object which smoothly floats through time and space, as historical linguistics based on philological material all too easily suggests. Rather, the transmission of language is discontinuous, and a language is recreated by each child on the basis of the speech data it hears.

Generative grammarians believe that each child is born with an ability which adults outgrow, the ability to extract grammatical rules from the speech he hears around him. This is what Kiparsky means when he says that a child "recreates" a language. This theory, which is still a matter of dispute, will be taken up again in Chapter Five. For the moment it will suffice to note that this is a rather different idea of the way languages change.

The major difference between the traditional approach to historical linguistics and the generative approach can perhaps best be stated in the following terms: it is not languages that change, but rather grammars. Thus the Elizabethan speaker who said, 'Left you early for London?' did not have the same set of rules in his grammar as does the modern speaker who says, 'Did you leave early for London?' Generative grammarians believe that languages change through the addition of rules to the grammar, the loss of such rules, a shift in the order of a set of rules, or the simplification of rules.

A very clear example has been pointed out by Elizabeth Traugott (1965). From a single deep structure composed of 'he left' and 'it was good', Modern English yields either of the following two sentences:

(4)   a. *That he left was good.*   (if *Nominalization* applies)

       b. *It was good that he left.*   (if *It-Extraposition* applies)

In Old English only 'It was good that he left' is possible, and the sentence 'That he left was good' would be ungrammatical. The linguist can then say that Old English did not have the rule of nominalization which results in sentences like 'That he left was good', and that this historical change can be accurately described by saying that this rule of *nominalization* has been added to the grammar of English.

Kiparsky has described a phonological change in the same manner. Modern English has a rule that says that vowels which are long in underlying structure appear as short vowels in surface structure when they are followed by two or more consonants. This rule can be written as follows:

(5) $V \rightarrow [- \text{LONG}] / \underline{\hspace{1cm}} CC$

This rule is responsible for pairs of forms like *keep/kept* and *sleep/slept*.

Old English had a rule that accomplished the same vowel-shortening, but the environment for application of the rule was three or more consonants rather than two. The rule was written as in (6) below, and accounted for forms like *godspell* whose underlying form had a long /o/.

(6) $V \rightarrow [- \text{ LONG}] / \underline{\quad\quad} CCC$

As you can see, the only difference between the Old English and the Modern English rule is that the Old English rule has been simplified.

Generative transformational linguists have been slow to take up significant work in historical linguistics, and the literature on the subject to date is rather limited. However, recently there have been indications that this situation, like grammars, has begun to change.

SUGGESTED READINGS FOR CHAPTER FOUR

GENERAL SOURCES ON LANGUAGE AND LINGUISTICS

BODMER, FREDERICK. *The Loom of Language*. New York: W. W. Norton and Company, Inc., 1944.

This book is a comprehensive source of interesting material on language and language history. It discusses the major language families of the world, writing systems, and many other subjects of importance. The style is completely nontechnical, and the book is as interesting as any novel.

CHADWICK, JOHN. *The Decipherment of Linear B*. Cambridge: Cambridge University Press, 1958.

This book is not about linguistics per se, but provides an excellent look at just what an extinct language is like and how scholars approach it.

WATERMAN, JOHN T. *Perspectives in Linguistics*. Chicago: University of Chicago Press, 1963.

This brief paperback discusses linguists and linguistics from the beginning up to (but not including) generative linguistics. It is intended for the non-specialist and is easy to understand. It will supply many more details about such topics as Grimm's Law and the neogrammarians.

TRADITIONAL HISTORICAL LINGUISTICS

BLOOMFIELD, LEONARD. *Language*. New York: Holt, Rinehart and Winston, Inc., 1933. Chapters 17–27.

One of the best introductions to traditional historical linguistics available. Clear, comprehensive, and easy to understand.

BROOK, G. L. *A History of the English Language*. New York: W. W. Norton and Company, Inc., 1958.

Although this book is not intended specifically for students of linguistics, it provides a very good description of the changes in English over the centuries and should be useful to anyone interested in historical linguistics.

GLEASON, H. A. "Genetic Relationship Among Languages." In *A Reader in Historical and Comparative Linguistics*, ed. Allan R. Keiler. New York: Holt, Rinehart and Winston, Inc., 1972, pp. 3–15.

An extremely good brief article on this subject, nontechnical and easy to understand.

HOCKETT, CHARLES F. *A Course in Modern Linguistics*. New York: The Macmillan Company, 1958, pp. 55–61.

Another classic introduction to traditional historical work. Somewhat more difficult than Bloomfield, but still well within the ability of the beginning student.

SAPIR, EDWARD. *Language*. New York: Harcourt Brace Jovanovich Inc., 1921 and 1949. Chapter 8, "Language as a Historical Product: Phonetic Law."

A brief and useful article in nontechnical style.

GENERATIVE TRANSFORMATIONAL HISTORICAL LINGUISTICS

KIPARSKY, PAUL. "Linguistic Universals and Linguistic Changes." In *Universals in Linguistic Theory*, eds. E. Bach and R. T. Harms. New York: Holt, Rinehart and Winston, Inc., 1968.

This article is written in technical style, but is very clear and not difficult to follow. It deals to a great extent with the question of the addition of rules and simplification of rules in a grammar.

TRAUGOTT, ELIZABETH CLOSS. "Diachronic Syntax and Generative Grammar." *Language* 41 (1965): 402–15.

This is a simple and comprehensive statement of the generative position on historical linguistics, with examples from various stages of English. It is technical, but the problems are so clearly explained that the minimal background provided by *What is Linguistics?* should be more than sufficient to enable the student to read and understand it.

A COMBINED SOURCE

KEILER, ALLAN R., ed. *A Reader in Historical and Comparative Linguistics*. New York: Holt, Rinehart and Winston, Inc., 1972.

This anthology contains a number of useful articles from both traditional and generative writers. The articles cited above by Gleason, Kiparsky, and Traugott are reprinted in this volume.

Psycholinguistics

The basic study of psycholinguistics is the relationship between human language and the human brain. This is an enormous problem to work with, and it covers many kinds and ranges of questions. It would not be possible to cover all of them, even briefly, in one chapter. What *is* possible, however, is to list a number of the questions that are most important to current psycholinguistic work, and then to discuss a few of these in some detail.

Among the questions the psycholinguist wants to answer are the following:

1. Is there any evidence for the reality of the grammatical theory proposed by transformationalists?

2. Is language innate in the human being, is it something inborn, or is it a learned activity?

3. What has happened in those cases where the language mechanism of speakers goes wrong due to injury or disease or some other factor? Can anything be done for such people?

4. Is the assumption that language is uniquely restricted to human beings correct, and if so, why?

Let's examine some of the work being done in the effort to answer these questions.

The Reality of Transformational Grammar

In previous chapters we have often used phrases such as "the operation of rules," "the production of language," "the output of the grammar," and so on. Nonlinguists reading such phrases have in the past mistakenly assumed that their use indicated a mechanistic view of human speech on the part of the linguists. There have been many complaints to the effect that the human being is not a machine, does not operate like a computer, and so on.

In response to these objections, it has become something of a tradition in linguistic texts to include a disclaimer to point out that just because the vocabulary of transformational grammar and the vocabulary of General Motors overlap a bit does not mean that the linguist cannot tell the difference between a human being and a production line.

This disclaimer is certainly a truthful one. Nobody, linguist or not, has very much knowledge about the linguistic structure of the human brain. No linguist for a moment wishes to claim that the brain contains some physiological representation of tree structures and Phrase Structure rules. It goes without saying that linguists do not believe that the human being who says 'Jump!' begins by checking a set of rules, noting that the deep structure of the sentence contains a 'you', subjecting that output to an examination which indicates that it meets the specifications for *Imperative Deletion*, and so on. Linguists make no claim that the steps outlined in transformational derivations are followed scrupulously by the native speaker like recipes for a casserole. However, even these nonclaims constitute a hypothesis of sorts. They amount to simply taking for granted that we cannot have any real knowledge about such matters.

Recently some psycholinguists have decided that it was time to test these assumptions. Granted that sentences are not put together like casseroles, still we should be able to determine whether the principles outlined by transformational grammar have any *psychological* reality.

In one experiment, linguists (Fodor and Bever, 1965) prepared a set of tape-recorded sentences. Over these sentences they superimposed a number of clicks. The subjects of the experiment listened to the taped sentences and were then asked to judge where the clicks had occurred. A subject would listen to a sentence and then write it down from memory, indicating by a slash his recollection of the position of the click.

The results of this study showed that no matter where the clicks were really located, the subjects' tendency was to hear them as if they were at a major constituent break in the sentence.

After the results of this experiment had been made public, there was some discussion as to whether the displacement of clicks might have been due not to constituent structures but rather to pauses in the sentences. In order to be certain about this, a new experiment was done (Garrett, Bever, and Fodor, 1966) using sentences which had identical sequences but different surface structures. For example, the following pair would show this difference:

(1)   a. *In her hope of leaving, Mary showed a lack of common sense.*

        b. *Her hope of leaving Mary showed a lack of common sense.*

This experiment maintained the results of the previous one.

These experiments show that there may be some evidence for the psychological reality of constituent structure *at the surface structure level.* This distinction is very important, since often the deep structure of a sentence is quite different from its surface structure. Consider the following sentence:

(2)   *It seems that Harry is stubborn.*

The deep structure proposed for this sentence is something like the following:

(3)

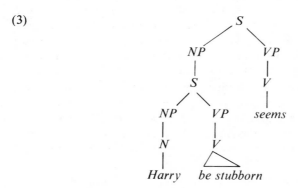

An experiment that shows subjects displacing clicks to a point immediately after surface structure constituent breaks tells us little or nothing about the possible psychological reality of a proposed deep structure like that shown in (3). Psycholinguists are now working with experiments that test for psychological reality of deep structures, and the results of these experiments will be of great interest.

The Innateness of Human Language

If you were asked how children acquire their language, what would you say? It is likely that you might say something like "he learns it from his parents" or "by imitating other people."

This view of language acquisition was once predominant in linguistics. In its most extreme form this theory claimed that the mind of the child is linguistically a blank slate, that the child imitates the speech of other people, and that he is reinforced in his imitations by his success in communicating. The idea that language is learned as a result of stimulus and reinforcement (the behaviorist approach) does have a limited amount of plausibility. It certainly is true that the child who asks for candy and gets it will have a strong tendency to remember the word "candy" correctly thereafter.

However, the evidence is overwhelmingly against anything more than this limited application. It is beyond the scope of this book to go into the technical discussion of the evidence, but it is easily found in the literature.

There is another theory about language acquisition called the *innateness* theory. This is the idea that a human being's language equipment is inborn rather than learned. One of the staunchest advocates of this theory is Eric Lenneberg. Lenneberg claims that man's language ability has been formed by evolution, and that there are crucial times for language development. He contends that the beginning of language in the child depends upon various maturational indices of the brain, and that once the physical maturation of the brain is complete—a condition he places at around puberty—the acquisition of language becomes much more difficult. Lenneberg states that ". . . the child abstracts regularities or relations from the language he hears, which he then applies to building up language for himself as an apparatus of principles" (Lenneberg, 1969). He contends that sometime in their early teens, children in effect outgrow their ability to do this.

This theory is strongly borne out by the facts. The amazing ease with which tiny children learn not only one, but even two or three languages, simply by virtue of being exposed to them, is well known. It does not seem to make a great deal of difference whether the child has the language presented to him in any systematic way; certainly no child is actively "taught" his native language by his parents in the form of lessons and exercises. The amount of talking the child hears, and the type of speech and speech situation vary radically from one child to another; nonetheless, all children learn their native tongue.

Further evidence for Lenneberg's theory is seen in the difficulty the adult has in learning a foreign language. He no longer has the ability to abstract a grammar from the raw data presented to him. Very few adults ever learn to speak a foreign language without an accent, but small children do so with ease.

There is a hypothesis in psycholinguistics, first proposed by Chomsky (1965) that every infant human being is born with something that has been called a *language acquisition device* (LAD for short). This does not mean that he is born with the grammar of his language already in his head—if that were so, the Russian child placed in a French home at birth and hearing only French thereafter would speak Russian, which of course is not the case. Instead, the LAD represents a set of strategies and principles that allow the child to figure out from the language data around him what the rules of his grammar are. This is not a random trial-and-error procedure, but a highly systematic one.

Consider a child who is brought up with English-speaking parents. He hears again and again sentences like 'John ate the apple', 'Mary saw the baby', 'Daddy fixed the car', and so on. From this data he extracts the basic principle that the usual order of English syntactic elements is subject-verb-object. (This is very different from the idea that he simply copies such sentences until he eventually learns to produce others like them.)

A second child, who grows up hearing Diegueño (an American Indian language), will hear sentences whose form is like 'Daddy the car fixed', 'John the apple ate', and so on. From this data he will extract and internalize the rule that his language has the syntactic order of subject-object-verb.

A child exposed to both languages is able not only to extract both rules but to keep straight which rule applies to which language.

Such facts indicate that a child does not speak some distorted approximation of adult speech, but rather bases his language acts upon a grammar of his own that he has constructed, from data presented to him, and by using the strategies that he was born with. Many interesting studies have been done by psycholinguists in this area, and there are particular differences between adult speech and child speech that can be shown to be completely systematic. For example, studies of the way children form English questions shows the following pattern:

(4)   a. *Why he is leaving?*

     b. *Who he is kissing?*

     c. *What he is doing?*

     d. *Where the truck is going?*

Such questions are not random "errors." What the child seems to be doing is moving the question word (*why*, *who*, etc.) to the front of the sentence, just as the adult does, but without following this step with the adult grammar rule that then inverts the subject and the verb. Later, as the child has more data made available to him, he will add the additional rule.

It is easy to see that children attempt to follow definite rules, by observing your own children or the children of your friends. Every adult has heard children say things like 'I goed', 'Mary singed', and so on. Some children even extend this to the point of saying, 'I wented'. They do this long before anyone has ever formally said to them anything like, "the sign of the English simple past tense is the suffix -*ed*. They have observed the facts about -*ed* for themselves, and as a productive strategy they apply it to all verbs. One of the most interesting things about this is that often a child who has at an earlier stage used the irregular past forms of verbs correctly will, upon having internalized the rule about -*ed*, suddenly switch to the incorrect forms.

Facts about child language acquisition constitute some of the strongest evidence for the universal grammar hypothesis. For example, we know that in every human society the child begins to talk by about eighteen months, and by the age of five he is able to converse in much the same way that adults do. The child's vocabulary is obviously more limited than the adult's, but it is clear that by roughly the age of five he has mastered the basic grammar of his native language. This is true no matter what the native language may be.

If some languages were "easier" than others, as has been traditionally assumed by students, we would expect to find the children who speak them beginning to speak at a significantly earlier age than the children who speak the "hard" languages. There is no evidence that this is true of any human language whatsoever. Even in the case where a child is exposed from birth to two or more languages and learns them all, there is no really significant difference in the timetable of language acquisition.

Disorders of the Language Mechanism

In this section we will discuss some of the knowledge available about human language when it is not functioning as it should. We are not concerned here with such problems as stuttering or the disorders commonly known as speech impediments, but rather with the large group of language disorders known by the cover term *aphasia*.

In aphasia there is an actual loss of language function. The causes of aphasia are many, the most common being severe organic disease of the brain, or traumatic injuries such as those caused by gunshot wounds and automobile accidents. The types of aphasia are also various, ranging from an impairment so minor as to be hardly noticeable to complete loss of all language ability, including speaking, reading, writing, and understanding. Many combinations are possible in aphasia; a patient may be able to read but not to write, or he may be able to understand speech but not to produce it, and so on. Given the central and urgent necessity for communication in all human beings, it is easy to see that aphasia is one of the most tragic illnesses, particularly since the patient is often in otherwise perfect health and in full possession of his intelligence, and is therefore agonizingly aware of his problems.

At one time it was thought that the brain could be divided up into specific areas, and that these could be specifically diagrammed the way countries are plotted on a map, with Area X responsible for loss of vocal speech, Area Y for loss of reading ability, and so on. There was a great deal of persuasive evidence for this type of classification, particularly from the effects of various kinds of brain surgery upon patients, and from the locations of brain lesions in particular types of disorders. This system is now being seriously questioned, however, in the light of much new evidence; and it appears that we cannot set up any correspondence between brain area and deficiency except in the most general way.

In his book *Psycholinguistics* (1970, pp. 119–20), James Deese states:

> Speech and language seem to be localized in the left cerebral hemisphere, the motor portion of which controls the right side of the body, for most people. . . . The linguistic dominance of the left hemisphere is not complete. Damage in the right cerebral hemisphere (which controls the muscles of the left side of the body) does produce some residual linguistic impairment, but the extent of the impairment is much less than for comparable left cortical damage.

Deese points out that in some left-handed people this situation may be reversed. Lenneberg feels that the localization of language functions in the left hemisphere of the brain is a postpuberty trait and that in the beginning both hemispheres are involved.

The facts about aphasia offer strong evidence for Lenneberg's claim. It is in fact true that although children may become aphasic just as do adults, they almost always recover completely from aphasic disorders and show no aphasic symptoms thereafter. This would seem to indicate that before some critical age it is possible for other areas of the brain to take over language functions formerly maintained by an area damaged by disease or injury. Or, on the other hand, it might indicate that the language function before puberty is distributed throughout the entire brain, and that specialization even to one hemisphere occurs much later. Aphasic recovery in adults shows a very wide range, instead of being a virtual certainty as it is for children.

Psycholinguists are extremely interested in the order in which children acquire various features of their speech. This is of great importance in aphasia, since it has been shown that aphasics lose phonological distinctions between sounds in exactly the reverse order that they are acquired by children learning to speak.

In the treatment of aphasia, since every facet of speech production and comprehension can be involved, it is easy to see that almost every bit of linguistic knowledge is of practical use and potentially of great value. The more we know about the language function in the normal human being, the more chance there is that we will be able to do something significant about cases of language impairment.

Animal Communication

The subject of animal "languages" has always been the source of intense controversy. A glance at any of the large indexes to periodical literature will show that there is a constant flood of articles on the subject, and that this flood is not confined to scholarly journals.

Some of this is no doubt simply due to human ego involvement. As human beings we are already aware that we share many, many characteristics with the other animals, particularly the mammals, and most particularly the primates. Books like Desmond Morris's *The Naked Ape* have brought forcibly to our attention the thinness of the line that separates *homo sapiens* from the gorilla, the chimpanzee, and the rest of the monkey tribes. We can go to any circus and watch these animals, dressed in human clothing, go through one routine after another that mocks our own behavior so closely as to be almost embarrassing. The larger primates are stronger than we are, quicker, and in many ways better equipped for survival. Faced with all this, it is not surprising that we want to cling to what appears to be the one sure evidence of our true superiority—our ability to use language.

At the other end of the scale we have the folklore of animal communication, the stories of talking crows and talking dogs, of horses that can count and spell, and the worrisome theory that the dolphin really has a language but is trapped in the isolation of its dependence upon the sea and its lack of hands and so cannot demonstrate its ability.

We can begin at the very bottom of the scale of animal communication, where it is certain that no actual language is being used. The skunk has a very clear and effective message to deliver—one that endures over an impressive period of time. The tenrec of Madagascar is a mammal, but it produces high-frequency sounds by rubbing together a group of small quills on its back, in what appears to be the mammalian equivalent of cricket noise. The squid in the depths of the ocean emits clouds of color to make it obvious that, like Garbo, it "wants to be alone." The beaver slaps its tail on the ground to warn its fellows of danger. All of these things are sounds, and sounds with meaning. But these meanings are like the meaning of a red traffic light—they are simply signals.

The famous "language of the bees" is confined entirely to the two subjects of food-hunting and house-hunting. There does not seem to be any mechanism for expansion of the set of signals involved. We cannot imagine bees carrying on any sort of conversation. They are simply transmitting facts about two specific situations, and this is not language.

The sounds made by birds are higher on the scale. Linguists have discovered that birds actually have dialects. The calls that American crows make to cause other crows to gather, or to scatter in times of danger, have been tape-recorded; when these recorded calls are played in American woods they have the same effect as live calls. But when they are played for French crows they are not understood, or are ignored entirely (Sebeok, in Fishman, 1968).

Obviously birds do communicate with each other, in the sense of transmitting various informative signals. Their vocal equipment is superb, and we know that many birds are capable of producing all the sounds of human speech. However, the very sophisticated mimicry done by birds like the mynah and the parrot is not true language because it can never be used creatively. No bird that has learned to utter the two sequences 'I see the girl' and 'the boy is here' will ever spontaneously produce the sequences 'I see the boy' and 'the girl is here'. No bird is able to negate a sentence or to ask a question that he has not been taught. We can be quite certain that the reason birds do not use language other than as signal and mimicry is that they simply cannot do so.

It is with the primates and the whales that we find ourselves with a genuine problem. How do we know, for example, that if we took a baby chimpanzee into a home and raised it like a human child, it would not learn to use human speech? This question becomes doubly crucial when we recall the claim that there is a critical point after which human children cannot learn to speak normally.

The obvious way to answer this question is to try it, and scientists have done just that. The first attempts were very disappointing. In one early experiment a chimpanzee spent six years being cared for just like a human baby, eating in a highchair, being dressed and fed and talked to, yet managed to acquire only four words in all that time.

However, linguists who had studied the construction of the human vocal tract and the mechanics of its use in speech pointed out that this was not a fair test. It happens that the vocal equipment of the chimpanzee is totally unsuited for human speech. On physiological grounds alone, the chimp can never learn human speech—it is *physically* impossible.

Then two scientists, R. Allen Gardner and Beatrice T. Gardner, decided to try a different approach. Again a baby chimpanzee (a female named Washoe) was raised in a home like a human child. But in this case the Gardeners tried to teach the animal to use sign language, thus bypassing her physical limitations. Given the manual dexterity of chimpanzees and their known intelligence, it was felt that this experiment would give the chimp a chance to show its real capability.

The Gardner experiment is still in progress, and the results so far have been interesting. At age five, Washoe had acquired the use of over eighty words, as compared with the four words that the chimpanzee described above learned to say in a similar amount of time. Of particular interest is a remark by the Gardners that "in discussing Washoe's early performance with deaf parents, we have been told that many of her variants of standard signs are similar to the baby-talk variants commonly observed when human children sign." (Gardner and Gardner, 1969). The Gardners also feel that Washoe understands many more signs than she actually produces.

Linguists cannot yet be certain about the speech abilities of the chimpanzee. Perhaps the work being done with Washoe will in time show us that the chimp *can* use human language but simply develops it at a slower rate than human children. Recent reports indicate that Washoe has not yet reached the limits of her language-learning ability, whatever those limits may prove to be. We will have to wait and see. But the results of the work with Washoe certainly indicate that we may have done the chimpanzees a severe injustice, much as if they had judged us to be stupid because we were not capable of swinging arm-over-arm through the trees.

The dolphins (really small toothed whales) are going to be more difficult to study in this regard than the primates. Obviously, you cannot take a dolphin into your home and raise it like a child. The dolphin is doubly handicapped physiologically for human speech; not only is its vocal equipment radically different from man's, but it lacks hands and thus cannot use sign language as Washoe has learned to do.

The most intensive work on dolphin communication has been done by John Lilly, author of *The Mind of the Dolphin*. In his Communication Research Institute in the Virgin Islands, he has constructed environments where it is possible for a human being and a dolphin to live together after a fashion. Lilly claims that not only does the dolphin have a language of its own, but it is willing and able to learn to communicate with man. Opinions of psycholinguists on the correctness of his claim range all the way from total rejection to a guarded support, and only time and more research will allow us to be certain. (This research is of course dependent on restraining man's present trend toward total destruction of these animals; if things go on as they have been, we may find all the whales, including the dolphins, extinct before we ever know if we could have talked together.)

Occasionally one hears linguistics—particularly in the areas of phonology, syntax, and semantics—described as an "ivory tower" discipline with no relation to the nonacademic outside world. This is not too surprising, since the practical applications of the theory in these three areas are not always immediately apparent. But this misconception is never directed toward psycholinguistics. It is obvious even to the individual who is totally uninterested in linguistics that the work of the psycholinguist extends into the most essential areas of man's daily life.

SUGGESTED READINGS FOR CHAPTER FIVE

BEVER, THOMAS G. "The Cognitive Basis for Linguistic Structure." In *Cognition and the Development of Language*. New York: John Wiley & Sons, Inc., 1970.
Of moderate difficulty.

CHURCH, JOSEPH. *Language and the Discovery of Reality*. New York: Vintage Books, 1966.
A nontechnical, clear discussion of such topics as child language acquisition and cognitive development.

DEESE, JAMES. *Psycholinguistics*. Boston: Allyn & Bacon, Inc., 1970.
This is a brief book, but superbly well done. It contains a summary of the methods and results of almost every important psycholinguistics study done in recent years, as well as a clear and comprehensive introduction to psycholinguistic theory. Highly recommended as the first book to read in this field.

FODOR, J., and T. BEVER. "The Psychological Reality of Linguistic Segments." *Journal of Verbal Learning and Verbal Behavior* 4 (1965): 414–20.
Somewhat technical but easy to understand.

GARDNER, R. ALLEN, and BEATRICE T. GARDNER. "Teaching Sign Language to a Chimpanzee." *Science* 165 (1969): 664–72.
This is the Gardner's highly readable account of their experiment in raising a chimpanzee in their household.

GARRETT, M., T. Bever, and J. FODOR. "The Active Use of Grammar in Speech Perception." *Perception and Psychophysics* 1 (1966): 30–32.
Slightly technical but easy to understand.

JAKOBSON, ROMAN. "Aphasia as a Linguistic Problem." In *On Expressive Language*, ed. H. Werner. Worcester, Mass.: Clark University Press, 1955, pp. 69–81.
Nontechnical and easy to understand.

LENNEBERG, E. *The Biological Foundations of Language*. New York: John Wiley & Sons, 1967.
This is the classic book on the innateness hypothesis for language. Of moderate difficulty.

——— "On Explaining Language." *Science* 165 (1969): 664–72.
An article on the innateness hypothesis; much less difficult than the book cited above, and a good introduction to it.

LOTZ, JOHN. "Linguistics: Symbols Make Man," In *Frontiers of Knowledge*, ed. L. White, Jr. New York: Harper and Brothers, 1956.
A very easy general introduction. Highly recommended.

SEBEOK, THOMAS A. "Communication in Animals and in Man: Three Reviews." In *Readings in the Sociology of Language*, ed. Joshua A. Fishman. The Hague: Mouton, 1968.
An interesting nontechnical article on animal communication.

VI

Sociolinguistics

Up to this point we have been discussing language primarily in the abstract, with little attention paid to the people who speak, how their lives are influenced by their language, and how their language is in turn affected by their lives. Can we justify the study of language in the abstract, as something divorced from the speaker? To answer that question, let's consider the following fragment of typical speech as used by an ordinary speaker like ourselves:

> What I did today—Johnny, will you stop that, please—I mean, did you notice how like every time you start to talk about something that's really important just about every damned thing imaginable happens? And some that aren't imaginable? Well, anyway . . . where was I? Oh, yes, I was telling you what happened. Well, it was about eight—or was it more like nine? I think it must have been eight, because the milk gets delivered at eight-fifteen, and I know it hadn't come yet because the dog always barks, so anyway, about eight I heard this incredible racket outside and I . . . .

This is the way most of us talk, except for occasions when we feel we are performing and therefore switch to hyper "correct" speech. Such situations include not only the obvious ones, as when we are giving a talk to a group, but also the first few minutes of conversation with strangers whose good opinion we are anxious to obtain, as in our first meeting with potential in-laws or in job interviews.

If your ordinary everyday manner of speaking is less like the sample above and more like the speech one hears on television or in the theatre, you may be one of the unusual people—one of the ideal speakers that linguists usually describe. But for most people, as you can observe by listening, the example given above is quite typical of spoken language.

Now, consider the problem of the linguist who tried to base his study of language upon such actual samples. Could he develop a theory to account for such speech? Could he find the underlying rules and principles that would bring order out of the apparent surface chaos?

Perhaps. No one has ever really tried. Although there have been some attempts at discourse analysis, there does not yet exist any developed theory that considers language over extended stretches of discourse and accounts in some principled way for its phenomena.

So far, linguists have constructed their basic theory by considering language as it might be, in isolation from the vagaries of performance, and they have been justified in doing so. Now, however, many linguists feel that it is time to move beyond this never-never land of perfect speech and consider the language of real people in the real world. This area of specialization is called *sociolinguistics*.

 William Labov, a contemporary sociolinguist, has said that "the social situation is the most powerful determinant of verbal behavior,"[1] and there is no reason to believe that he has exaggerated.

Like any other linguist, the sociolinguist begins with an *idiolect*—i.e., with the language spoken by some one individual. But he will then move not inward to further analysis within the idiolect, but outward to investigate the interactions between this idiolect and its social context. He wants to know what effects the idiolect has on the culture, and vice versa. In this chapter we will examine some of these effects as they have been studied by sociolinguists.

Etiquette-Based Language

We in the United States live in a country that is called "the land of the free," and that is described as a democracy with equal opportunity for every man and without class distinctions. Our language is intended to reflect this image, and we therefore pride ourselves on the absence from our speech of

[1] In "The Logic of Nonstandard English," a paper presented at the Georgetown University 20th Annual Round Table Meeting on Linguistics and Language Studies, 1969.

honorific terms like 'milord', 'milady', 'your grace', 'master', 'your worship', 'your highness', and so on. Our most prestigious terms are perhaps 'Mister', 'Mrs.', and 'Miss'; with the new term 'Ms.'—intended to apply to all women as 'Mister' does to all men—fast becoming an established member of this set. ('Ms.' seems an unfortunate choice to southern speakers like myself, who have always had in their speech a morpheme 'Miz', pronounced just like the new 'Ms'. but restricted to married women only.) There are also the terms 'Sir' and 'Ma'am', but these are rapidly falling into obsolescence except in the military, particularly for speakers under the age of twenty.

At the very bottom of our language etiquette scale, on the other hand, we primarily find sequences like the following, spoken in a loud and unmistakably contemptous tone:

$$\text{Hey there,} \begin{Bmatrix} boy \\ kid \\ lady \end{Bmatrix} \text{—where do you think you're going?}$$

There are languages, however, where linguistic etiquette is not just a matter of choosing among a handful of honorifics and pejoratives of address. As reported by Burling (1970), the Javanese language is divided into at least three social levels of style, and all speakers must continually adjust their speech to these levels. Every sentence uttered by a Javanese speaker unambiguously indicates his own estimation of his social status relative to the person he is speaking to. The Javanese word 'to eat' has three forms:

lowest social level	*mangan*
middle level	*neda*
prestige level	*dahar*

To use the word *magnan* for the phrase 'to eat' when speaking to someone who is actually your social equal is to insult him. As you can see, this is not just a matter of tacking on a chunk here and there, as in the parody, "will the honorable guest please sit on this unworthy chair." For speakers of English it is difficult to see how the Javanese speaker can forever be keeping these three levels straight in his head and making choices among them without radically slowing down and inhibiting his speech.

And there immediately comes to mind the problem of language choice when there is no live listener present. What sort of speech is to be used by a television news commentator, for example, who is presumably speaking to the whole of the Javanese people? It happens that there is another language, Indonesian, which is spoken in this same area. Indonesian has no elaborate system of class differentiation, and it is therefore the language of the mass media. Javanese speakers also say that they automatically switch to Indonesian for business or politics, since for such situations Javanese does not seem appropriate or convenient.

The Multilingual Nation

The multilingual nation is always a source of sociolinguistic problems, although the intricacy of the Javanese situation is rather unusual. These problems will ordinarily remain minor in a country where there is a high level of wealth and technological sophistication. For example, Switzerland manages nicely with a population which has as its languages French, German, Italian, and Romansch.[2]

In Paraguay there are two native languages, Spanish and Guaraní. Spanish is considered the official language and is taught in the schools. Guaraní, the native Indian language spoken in the rural areas, should typically have become a looked-down-upon minority speech. In actual fact, however, this has not happened. There is a growing movement for equal status for both languages, seemingly without any serious opposition from those who have in the past favored Spanish. Paraguay has a language academy which not only establishes standards for the Guaraní language but is now also engaged in preparing teaching materials to introduce Guaraní into the schools of the country.

What happens, however, in troubled countries like India, where an enormous population speaks such a variety of different languages that sometimes neighboring villages speak mutually incomprehensible languages or dialects? What happens in a situation like that represented by the former French colonies in Africa, where a dominant political and economic group attempts to impose its own language by force upon the native populations? What happens when a particular national language becomes a symbol of national pride and identity, as in Ireland? What happens when a powerful national group gains economic control of some language area, and it becomes desirable for the people who live there to speak some approximation of the other language, at least for business purposes?

We can consider a number of possibilities that exist in such situations. First, we will take up the topic of the *lingua franca*.

Lingua Franca

When the Crusaders went off to the Holy Land, they came from many different countries and spoke many different languages. In order to solve

---

[2] This linguistic calm is not always the rule; consider the current strife in the Canadian province of Quebec, where the French-speaking population and its English-speaking counterpart are struggling for a position of dominance.

their communication problems they chose to use as a common language the "French language," by which they meant Provençal, the language of an area of southern France. From this there comes the term *lingua franca*, now used to identify the various kinds of languages that may be used when diverse linguistic groups must find a common medium of communication.

A lingua franca may be a natural language—i.e., the native language of some group of people. Both Greek and Latin have served as lingua francas in the past, and Swahili seems a likely candidate in much of Africa today. However, this is not the most usual situation, since it is not easy either to agree upon a single language for this purpose or to induce everyone to learn it rapidly enough.

It is more common for a lingua franca to be what is known as a *pidgin* language. The definitions and uses of the term pidgin vary in the literature, and you should be prepared for this variation when you consult the supplemental readings listed in the bibliography. In this book, however, we will define pidgin as a mode of speech that is not anyone's native language, but which can be demonstrated to have developed from at least one such language.

Typically, a pidgin retains a large portion of the lexicon and phonology of the language from which it has developed, but it radically simplifies the syntax of that language. Such things as grammatical gender distinctions, elaborate compound verb tenses, and complicated systems of pronouns are ordinarily casualties of pidginization.

When people speaking a pidgin are for one reason or another isolated from other language communities, it may happen that a new generation will be born which has no other language except the pidgin. A language like this, that has been a pidgin but has now become a native language, is called a *creole*. As can be easily seen, the exact point at which a pidgin stops being pidgin and becomes creole may be difficult to determine. In some cases, as with Jamaican Creole, we find the process being reversed; Jamaican Creole, probably because of education and exposure to the mass media, is losing its creole status and becoming a true dialect of English instead.

There is a language spoken in northern Canada which seems to be the result of extensive contact between French and the Cree Indian language. It is difficult to say whether this language, called Métis, is a pidgin or a creole. It offers some excellent examples of the results of such language contact, however, and we will look at a few of them.[3]

French has an impressive array of interrogative and relative pronouns, among which are *qui* and *que*. This pair of pronouns is phonologically identical for both interrogative and relative, and takes part in a complicated system of grammatical distinctions. A speaker of French who wishes to use

---

[3] For the material on Métis I am indebted to Robert Papen, a linguist at the University of California, San Diego, who has done field work with the language.

these words correctly must keep in mind whether the pronoun refers to a person or a thing, and whether it represents the subject or the object of a sentence; furthermore, these two distinctions do not apply uniformly to the two homophonous pronouns. In addition, there are rules governing word order arrangements with *qui* and *que* that must also be taken into account. The speakers of Métis have bypassed some of these distinctions by choosing another French pronoun, *quoi*, to serve all the functions of *que*. *Quoi* simplifies matters even further since it is an invariable form. Compare the following sentences, which show the standard French and its Métis equivalent:

(1)   French: *Vous voyez **ce que** je veux dire.*
       Métis: *Vous voyez **quoi** je veux dire.*
                (You see *what* I want to say.)

(2)   French: *Qu'est-ce que c'est?*
       Métis: *Quoi c'est?*
                (*What* is it?)

In this case we see Métis simplifying the syntax of French, while at the same time retaining an item from the French lexicon.

Another Métis example shows a process which is not necessarily a matter of syntactic simplification, but rather of the imposition of Cree syntax upon French lexical items. Cree, like many other American Indian languages, has a mechanism for indicating the possessive which produces expressions translatable as 'John his-hat', 'Mary her-lamb', and so on. The following example shows the effect of this pattern in Métis:

(3)   French: *les neveux de Maman*
                (the nephews of Mama)
       Métis: *Maman ses neveux*
                (Mama her nephews)

Dialect Diversity

It is important to keep in mind that dialect diversity is not restricted just to minority groups, although that may be where we see the most striking examples of the phenomenon.

The United States shows a remarkable range of dialect differences. These differences are not confined just to such things as whether one says *skillet* or *frying pan*, or *movies* or *picture show*. There are also systematic underlying phonological and syntactic differences. Let's examine one example of such a syntactic difference—that which is found in the Ozark dialect spoken throughout a large area of the American Midwest (Elgin, 1972).

The linguist Paul Postal has proposed that there is a constraint on English grammar, known as the *Crossover Constraint*, which forbids any movement transformation interchanging two noun phrases which are co-referential. To see what this means consider the following:

(4) *Mary$_i$ shot Mary$_i$.*

If we apply the *Passive* transformation to this sequence the result will be the following:

(5)   a. *Mary$_i$ shot Mary$_i$.*
          1   2
                                              Apply *Passive* →
       b. *Mary$_i$ was shot by Mary$_i$.*
          2   1

If we then apply *Reflexive* as we must, the final sentence is:

(6) *Mary was shot by herself.*

It happens that for Ozark speakers this is a perfectly good sentence and fully grammatical. For most English speakers, on the other hand, it constitutes a violation of the Crossover Constraint and is an ungrammatical sentence of English.

Another difference between Ozark speakers and those who speak the majority dialect called Standard American English lies in the interpretation of various prepositional phrases. For example, consider the following sentence:

(7) *John was told to sit by Hermione.*

In this writer's dialect this sentence has to be synonymous with:

(8) *John was told to sit beside Hermione.*

In the standard dialect, on the other hand, although the interpretation in (8) is possible, the sentence is ordinarily considered to be equivalent to:

(9) *It was Hermione who told John to sit.*

The investigation of the differences between various dialects of one language is one of the sub-areas of sociolinguistics, and has a particular subgroup, the dialect geographers, who concentrate entirely upon the isolation of such differences in geographical terms.

Differences of Style

Each of us speaks in a way that is characteristic of himself alone, but which can be said to belong to a set of idiolects that in turn constitute a dialect of a given language. What about the idiolect, however? Within its boundaries— i.e., within the speech of a single individual—is everything always completely uniform?

Of course not. If you compare the way you speak to your boss with the way you speak to your children, or, if you are under twenty, the way you speak to your peers with the way you speak to most adults, you will realize at once that this is manifestly false.

There are various sociolinguistic signals of this type which we all learn to recognize as children. For example, any child who does not know the difference between "Bobby, I want to talk to you" and "Robert Allen Jamison, I want to talk to you" is badly in need of sociolinguistic instruction.

Many differences of style are not systematic. They can be attributed to such things as health, state of intoxication, degree of emotional excitement, and the like. When a style difference is systematic, however, it is called a *register*. Thus, a child may customarily speak in one register of language at school and in another at home.

We find a type of "school register" permanently incarcerated in readers for children, where all the boys and girls appear to be unaware that the English language contains any contractions. Little boys playing ball are portrayed as saying, "I am tired. It is almost dinnertime. I am going home." This is not the way real children speak, nor is it the way any native speaker speaks English, except for characters in primers.

One dialect of English that we all speak at times has been described by sociolinguist David DeCamp as marked by the feature [POMPOUS]. Although perhaps more characteristic of university professors and clergymen, it is also typical of people who have just discovered that they are talking *to* a professor or clergyman. A typical example of [+ POMPOUS] speech is the following:

> It appears that we shall be able to commence this morning's activities in a moment.

Another area of sociolinguistics specializes in the study of slang and the argots of professional and other groups. Recently there has been a tremendous upsurge of interest in the special slang of the drug culture, with a resulting—and extremely curious—reflection in the American mass media.

What significance is there, for example, in the fact that to "turn on" with drugs can mean a long prison sentence, yet advertising has made it a household term in connection with almost every product from Avis to Zenith, all of which are claimed to "really turn you on." The sociolinguist is interested in the interactions between groups within the culture that are reflected in language phenomena of this type.

The International Auxiliary Language

People have always agreed that it would be wonderful if there were one international language that everybody spoke. There does not seem to be any dispute about the validity of this idea in the abstract. We have only to look at the endless expense and complication of the translation and interpreting apparatus at the United Nations to see a cardinal example of the inefficiency of the current linguistic scene.

However, the consensus disappears when it comes to actually agreeing upon such a language. An international auxiliary language would be a lingua franca for the whole world, and as such would be a tremendous benefit for mankind—but which language is to serve? If you speak English you may say "English, of course," but a moment's reflection will show you that if you were Chinese you would select Chinese, if you were Russian you would select Russian, and so on, human egos being what they are.

In an attempt to get around this problem, many artificial languages have been proposed. One of the first such constructed languages was that proposed by Bishop John Wilkins in 1668, a language he claimed was based upon mathematical symbols and scientific principles. His effort has been followed since that time by several hundred other competing proposals. We are going to examine perhaps the best-known one, the language called Esperanto.

Esperanto was devised by Dr. Ludwig Zamenhof of Poland. Estimates of the number of Esperanto speakers today range from a minimum of several hundred thousand on up. There is an Esperanto headquarters—the Universal Esperanto Association in Rotterdam—with member associations in eighty-three countries. There are more than 30,000 books available now in Esperanto, many of which are original works in the language rather than translations. In a number of countries (for example Italy, Austria, and the Netherlands) Esperanto is taught in the schools as a foreign language on a basis similar to that of any other foreign language. It has been extremely popular in Japan and China; and even in the United States, where it has been less successful, there is a large and very active Esperanto Association.

Esperanto has only a handful of grammar rules. Word order is virtually free. After as little as two hours of instruction, adults are able to begin using Esperanto with an amazing degree of fluency, and children who have had half a dozen lessons in Esperanto can begin corresponding with Esperanto-using children in other countries.

Given all these advantages, what keeps the people of the world from unanimously adopting Esperanto as an international language? Look at the following representative selection (from *El Afriko*, an Esperanto reader). You will see at once what the problem is.

> Preskaŭ 40 milionoj da homoj loĝas en la baseno de la rivero Nilo. Dum miloj de jaroj, la bonstato de tiuj egiptoj kaj sudanoj dependis de la fluo de la Nilo. Dum sezonoj, kiam la pluvofalo en la sudaj montoj estis granda, la "nilanoj" prosperis.

> Almost 40 million people live in the basin of the river Nile. Through thousands of years the well-being of every Egyptian and Sudanese has depended on the flow of the Nile. During seasons when the rainfall in the southern mountains was heavy, the "people of the Nile" prospered.

As you can see, although Esperanto is proposed as international, it is based almost entirely upon the Indo-European languages. Its vocabulary is all very well if you are French or German or Spanish or American or even Russian or Greek—all these languages being represented among the Esperanto lexical items—but what if you are a speaker of Cherokee or Swahili or Tibetan or Samoan? For you Esperanto will still be the foreign language of a dominant social and political group.

Just what the fate of Esperanto will be is difficult to say. At the moment it is seeing a slow but steady gain in popularity. It is interesting to note that there are now a number of people who spoke Esperanto as their first language. This has happened in cases where one member of a marriage spoke Japanese, for example, and the other French, with the only shared language in the home being Esperanto. Such speakers are called *denaska* (from birth) Esperantists.

The sociolinguists have not as yet turned their full attention to Esperanto or to any of the other proposed international languages. When they do, it will be possible to examine linguistic analyses of these languages and to study reports of their possible impact in countries where they are widely used.

Sign Language

One of the most interesting areas of sociolinguistic phenomena is the sign language used by the deaf. It has been traditional to forbid children the use of sign language, on the grounds that it emphasizes their deafness. Thus, until very recently, deaf children were not taught sign by their teachers but learned it from each other in secret—it was in fact an "underground" form of communication. In the classroom these children had to try to learn entirely from lipreading and from written materials.

It is encouraging that in the United States there are now a number of schools where not only is the use of sign taught and encouraged, but there is an attempt at the concept of "total communication." What this means is that teachers and students use all available means of communicating—i.e., sign, lipreading, written materials, and anything else that is useful.

Sign is not an international language. It seems that it could be (consider the sign language of the American Indians, which was truly pan-Indian and could be understood by speakers of all languages), but even American sign and British sign are based upon entirely different systems.

To make clear why this should be so, it is necessary to point out that sign language does not consist of spelling out the words of the oral language. There is a finger-spelling alphabet, which is available for introducing new words between speakers, for communicating proper names, and so on, but true signing does not consist of finger spelling at all, nor does it consist of pantomime. It is a true language, with its own syntax and semantics, and much work is now being done with it by linguists.

There are an estimated 250,000 Americans and Canadians using the ASL (American Sign Language) system.[4] In the ASL system, each sign is based upon the following three factors:

1. The place the sign is made (near the eye, against the chest, etc.)

2. The configuration of the hand (with fingers spread wide, a closed fist, etc.)

3. The action of the hand (a motion away from the speaker, toward the speaker, etc.)

Recently a dictionary of ASL has been published that attempts to set down all the signs of the language in terms of these three factors, by using an inventory of fifty-five symbols—twelve for the location of the sign, eighteen for the hand configuration, and twenty-three for the action of the hand. This first comprehensive attempt to make sign accessible to all who wish to study it should prove very valuable in furthering the acceptance of ASL as a valid method for communication by the deaf.

An interesting area of research which we have not had space to take up

[4] William C. Stokoe, Jr., *A Dictionary of American Sign Language on Linguistic Principles* (Washington, D.C., Gallaudet College Press, 1965).

in this chapter is that of the bilingual speaker, and the many questions as to just how he learns, how his language activities differ from those of the unilingual speaker, and so on. Similarly, there exist speakers who are called *bimodal*[5] because they use both sign and vocal speech as native speakers. In most cases these individuals are the nondeaf children of deaf parents, who have learned sign as their native language in the home but have learned the language of the speaking community around them as well.

Sociolinguistics, like psycholinguistics, moves beyond the purely theoretical to the practical. Because almost every human situation is a sociolinguistic situation, the investigations of sociolinguists are relevant to all of us in our daily life, in our work, at home, and wherever we use language in our contacts with other human beings.

SUGGESTED READINGS FOR CHAPTER SIX

BROWN, R., and A. GILMAN. "The Pronouns of Solidarity and Power." In *Style in Language*, ed. T. Sebeok. Cambridge: M.I.T. Press, 1960, pp. 253–76.

A sociolinguistic analysis of the use of pronouns of address in English, French, German, and Italian. The article is nontechnical and easy to understand.

BURLING, ROBBINS. *Man's Many Voices: Language in Its Cultural Context*. New York: Holt, Rinehart, and Winston, Inc., 1970.

This is one of the most interesting books on language in culture available. It is technical at times, but all material is carefully explained, and nowhere does the difficulty become a barrier to the reader's understanding. Excellent chapters on anthropological linguistics (an area not dealt with in *What Is Linguistics?*), analysis of kinship and color term systems, dialect diversity in India, the current status of investigation of Black English, and many other valuable topics. Highly recommended.

FISHMAN, JOSHUA A., ed. *Readings in the Sociology of Language*. The Hague: Mouton, 1968.

An excellent anthology. Particularly valuable are the following articles, none of them technical or difficult: "Linguistic Etiquette," by Clifford Geertz; "The Urbanization of the Guaraní Language: A Problem in Language and Culture," by Paul L. Garvin and Madeleine Mathiot; and "Lingua Francas of the World," by William J. Samarin.

MCDAVID, RAVEN. "Postvocalic -*r* in South Carolina: A Social Analysis," In *American Speech* 23 (1948): 194–203. Also in *Language in Culture and Society: A Reader in Linguistics and Anthropology*, ed. Dell Hymes. New York: Harper & Row, Publishers, 1964.

One of the landmark articles in sociolinguistic analysis of phonological phenomena. Not difficult.

[5] For this term I am indebted to Ursula Bellugi-Klima.

VII

Stylistics

The word "stylistics" as it is used in this chapter refers to the application of the principles of linguistics to literary language. In reading linguistic literature you will come across a number of terms that have to do with one or another facet of stylistics; these include *prosody*, *poetics*, *metrics*, *rhetoric*, *literary analysis*, and perhaps others.

In the past, and even today, the analysis of literary language has been hampered by an attitude that is a strange combination of reverence, fear, and mysticism. This is the attitude that would put all literature, and particularly poetry, on a pedestal, with a large and garish sign that would read DO NOT TOUCH. This attitude has led to the idea that literary language is the product of divine inspiration and therefore can only be admired, but never understood. And it is from this attitude that we get such phrases as "poetic license," understood by many people as the poet's right to do anything at all with words and call it poetry. Examination of the work of experimental writers has reinforced this "no rules" approach, even for those in whom it has destroyed all idea of reverence—this is the "A-Monkey-At-The-Zoo-Could-Do-It" school.

Those linguists who have been willing to do literary analysis have gone about it in a number of ways. There is the listing of rhetorical devices, for example, or the counting of metric patterns. There is the attempt to apply the theory of music—and even musical notation—to the analysis of poetry and rhythmic prose. There is the sort of statistical nit-picking that takes a text and tells us how many *r*'s it contains and how many *o*'s and attempts to derive some general principles from this information. (Here the analyst is really barking up the wrong tree, since, as has been pointed out by the linguist Bierwisch, you could take any text and rearrange its letters to produce many other texts, and all would contain the same percentages of *r*'s and *o*'s.)

To describe and characterize literary language by any of these methods has its good points. It is like our usual method of describing a house, for example. We say that the house is of such and such a size, has a red roof, is one story high and has a chimney, is built of redwood, and so on. When we get through doing this we have a mental picture of the house, but we could not possibly build one. We do not yet have any conception of the structural principles behind all this apparatus of red roofs and chimneys; and if we tried to reproduce the house in terms of our understanding, it would immediately fall down. We leave the building of houses to the experts, those who understand the principles of space and stress and support.

Since linguists are experts on language, they should be able to get beyond this surface literary analysis—or they should disqualify themselves and say that their expertness is confined to nonliterary language. This last alternative bears discussing.

There would be two reasons for excluding stylistics from linguistics. The first, the one that is heard most often, is that literary language is "above" analysis. Implicit in this is the idea that we somehow weaken or debase such language by analyzing it. This is perhaps more a matter of value judgment than of scientific judgment, but it is difficult to see how anything that adds to our understanding of a literary work could possibly do it harm. No one claims that we weaken Van Gogh's painting by learning what ingredients he used in the pigments; it would be ludicrous to claim that an understanding of the progressions and modulations Beethoven used in his Ninth Symphony would make that symphony less powerful. It is perhaps because although not all of us can paint or compose music, every single one of us can use words; and in order to account for the admiration we feel for literary works, we find it necessary to preserve some distance between "our words" and "the words in books."

If we can dispense with the idea that literary language is too frail to bear our bumbling touch—and surely we can—we then have another, and more legitimate, reason to contend with.

This is the claim that it is beyond the power of linguistics to describe literary language. This is not a value judgment. If it is true, it is a simple statement of fact and would constitute an incontrovertible reason for leaving all such language alone. But is it true? What is entailed in making such a claim?

Linguistics is the *systematic* description of language, remember. It is the process of finding the rules that underlie the surface structures, and of accounting for those surface structures in a principled way. If we cannot do this for literary language it can only mean one of two things: (1) writers do not have an ordinary human brain, and therefore their language is beyond the capacity of ordinary humans to describe; (2) writers do not know what they are doing, the effects they achieve are at best accidental, and therefore cannot be systematically analyzed.

The first of these two reasons can be eliminated at once, as anyone who has spent a little time with writers will agree. The second, however, is open to empirical testing. Is it true? If a way can be found to describe literary language as explicitly as we describe the language of ordinary discourse, then it is simply false. And this is what linguists are now trying to do.

Let's consider a very famous (and much-analyzed) line by E. E. Cummings: "He danced his did." We all know, because we are native speakers of English, that this is not an acceptable sentence of ordinary discourse. It seems to be structurally parallel to sentences like 'He launched his boat', 'He cooked his lunch', and so on, all of which can be produced by the set of Phrase Structure rules we have seen before:

(1) $S \rightarrow NP\ VP$

   $NP \rightarrow (Det)\ N$

   $VP \rightarrow V\ (NP)$

However, there is no analysis of English that will allow us to generate 'he danced his did' by applying these three rules. What must we do, therefore?

There have been two major transformational approaches to this problem in the past. The first says that there is an ordinary grammar of English and there is a literary one, and that the literary grammar of English may be said to contain a rule that will generate 'he danced his did'. The second says that each literary work is to be looked upon as a separate *dialect* of English, and that within the dialect of the particular poem by Cummings there is a rule like the following, which will generate the necessary string:

(2) $NP \rightarrow (Det)\ V$

The point of both of these approaches, of course, is to prevent the language of literature from having an unwanted effect upon the language of ordinary discourse. That is, if you are going to let Cummings generate 'he danced his did' and call it grammatical, how are you to prevent thousands of other such sentences from being generated in everyday language?

It is possible, however, that neither the separate grammar nor the separate dialect approach is really needed. This is very good, since either one would lead to an enormous complication of English grammar. Let's consider how this complication could be avoided.

The Recognition of Literary Language

First of all, what *is* literary language? The *Iliad* is, of course, and the Gettysburg Address is, and the work of Robert Frost is. But this is not really saying anything, it is just making a list. We recognize literary language in a number of ways, and we will mention just two of them here.

The first indication that language is literary language is the presence of certain *recognition conventions*, among which are such things as the text having a title, being set off in the center of a page, being bound between two covers, containing rhyme or a metric pattern, and the like. Secondly, we often note the presence of *deviant* structures, for example, in poetry and some prose works like the novels of Gertrude Stein, which show a marked degree of deviance, while much prose shows very little.

Literary language, then, is found in plays, novels, poetry, short stories, textbooks, sermons, advertisements, and many other writings—in anything that is not just a list (like a telephone directory), not purposeless nonsense (like the language of delirium), and not ordinary discourse.

Once literary language has been identified as such, the grammar marks it with the feature [POETIC] from beginning to end. We can then write grammatical rules which are of the form, "Given a sequence of language which is marked [+ POETIC] . . . " and go on to describe what happens next.

One of the most obvious rules that could be written, and one that would not require any transformational apparatus whatsoever, is the following:

(i) **Given a sequence of language which is marked [+ POETIC], selectional restrictions are suspended.**

Selectional restrictions are those mechanisms of the grammar which insure that the *NP* object of the verb 'to eat' will not be something inedible like 'liberty' or 'tennis match'. To see what this would mean, consider the following line, again from E. E. Cummings:

(3)   *I am going to utter a tree.*

Now the selectional restrictions of English would mark this sequence as ungrammatical in ordinary discourse because the transitive verb 'to utter' cannot have 'a tree' as its object. They would allow us to produce all of the following sequences, but not the Cummings one:

(4)   a. *I am going to utter a word.*

     b. *I am going to utter a sentence.*

     c. *I am going to utter a syllable.*

As you can see, a great deal of literary language can be accounted for at once by the simple mechanism specified in (i).

We know, however, that there is a vast amount of literary language that cannot be described so easily, and that may require the addition of some transformational rules. We are now going to consider such a transformation.

A Literary Transformation of English

Linguists know that literary language uses all the transformations that ordinary language does. Questions are formed in the same way, negation is indicated in the same way, as in any other language. The sentence 'Patricia wants to leave' must in literary language have come from a deep structure in which there were two instances of 'Patricia', and cannot be interpreted as 'Patricia wants John to leave'. However, at the point where literary language begins to deviate from the standard set by the grammar of ordinary discourse, we can expect to find one or more transformations that apply *only* in the context [+ POETIC].

The literary transformation we want to examine, for purposes of illustration, is called *Overlap Deletion*. In much the same way that the transformations of ordinary discourse operate, this transformation deletes one of two identical sequences from a string of literary language. Example (5) below shows the operation of *Verb Phrase Deletion*, a transformation of ordinary language.

(5)   a. *Bill tried to climb a tree, and then Mary tried to climb a tree, too.*

     b. *Bill tried to climb a tree, and then Mary tried, too.*

One of the original sequences 'to climb a tree' has been deleted from (5b). Now consider (6), which is a perfectly plausible English poetic line:

(6)   *I have seen you have seen me.*

The deeper structure shown in (7) underlies this line, just as (5a) underlies (5b).

(7)   *I have seen you / you have seen me.*

The effect of the transformation is to combine two original strings, the last lexical item of one and the first lexical item of the next being phonologically identical, into a single string that is linked by only one instance of the lexical item. That this transformation can operate only when the two items are exactly identical phonologically is easily shown; for example, consider (8), which is structurally parallel to (7):

(8)   *I have seen him / he has seen me.*

There is no way to apply *Overlap Deletion* to this sequence. Neither of the two possible sequences resulting would allow the poet to preserve the original two strings, as shown in (9):

(9)   a. *I have seen him has seen me.*

      b. *I have seen he has seen me.*

This transformation is very common in English poetry, both in its present form and in a somewhat more restricted form, the familiar process known as double syntax. The difference between the two processes lies in the fact that double syntax requires that the resulting *combined* sequence be a grammatical string for English. For example:

(10) *I know she has done something*
      she should not have done.

Sentence (10) can be read as the result of applying *Overlap Deletion* to the following sequence:

(11) *I know she has done something*
      she has done something she should not have done.

Both the first line of (10) and the combination of both lines of (10) are grammatical sequences of English. This is not true of (6) however, as shown by the following:

(12) a. *I have seen you.*

      b. **I have seen you have seen me.*

Work done on this transformation has shown that it can be very precisely formulated, that it is not applied in a random manner, and that it is in fact quite rigidly constrained. What concerns us here, however, is not the formal structure of this transformation, but the fact that it does not require any new or different grammatical apparatus. We already need the process of deletion under identity for the grammar of ordinary English discourse. It is therefore necessary only to extend this principle of deletion under identity to literary language.

There are other literary transformations, the discussion of which is beyond the scope of this text. They again are simply extensions of principles of the ordinary discourse grammar. There is the literary substitution transformation (analogous to the pronominalization transformations of English), for example; it is this transformation that is responsible for puns and parody.

There are two characteristics that all literary transformations must have:

a. All literary transformations must follow the application of all nonliterary transformations.

b. All literary transformations are optional.

It is in (b) that the reality of "poetic license" is to be found. That is, there could never be an instance in which the poet could not freely choose between the alternatives of (13).

(13) a. *I have seen you*
           you have seen me.
       b. *I have seen you*
           have seen me.

For literary transformations, as for all others, there remains the primary constraint that no transformation may be allowed to change meaning. It is obvious, however, that for literary language the performance factor is going to be much higher than it is for ordinary discourse, since the writer is in effect attempting to introduce systematic deviance into his language—and the skill with which this is done is going to vary from individual to individual.

If, as seems likely, it is possible to demonstrate that all the processes of literary language are already present in ordinary language, there is no need to propose a separate grammar for literature. Obviously this would be a great simplification, since separate grammars would require that there be two of everything. For example, there would have to be a *Passive* for ordinary discourse and a *Passive* for literary language, a *Reflexive* transformation for each, and so on. These pairs of transformations would be absolutely identical except with regard to the language context in which they applied. Then, in addition, the literary grammar would have to contain all the optional literary transformations that are forbidden for ordinary discourse. This would be a very wasteful system.

Metrics

We are all familiar with the concept of meter. We begin our experience with meter, for the most part, with some sequence like the following:

(14) BAA BAA BLACK SHEEP
     HAVE YOU A-NY WOOL (*pause*)
     YES SIR YES SIR
     THREE BAGS FULL (*pause*)

The baby who is exposed to (14) doesn't know anything about metrics, but he knows what he likes, and he certainly is aware of the rhythm of the sequence. Babies make this awareness very evident by clapping their hands or jumping up and down in perfect time with the verse.

When we are a little older we go to school and learn about something called *iambic pentameter*. In most cases we learn this in a way that makes us carry about in our heads forever a deadly memory that is represented by (15):

(15) da DA/da DA/da DA/da DA/da DA

Now this is all very well. There is nothing intricate or complicated about the meter of nursery rhymes like "Baa, Baa, Black Sheep," nor about the kind of verse line that can be accurately represented by the formula of (15). All of the following lines, for example, could be analyzed as faithful to that formula:

(16) a. I *saw* the *ships* sail *in* on *Christ*mas *Day*.

                                           —Traditional

     b. When *forty* w*int*ers *shall* be*siege* thy *brow* . . .

                                           —Shakespeare

     c. Shall *I* com*pare* thee *to* a *sum*mer's *day* . . .

                                           —Shakespeare

No one, however, can spend more than a few hours reading English poetry without becoming aware that iambic pentameter, which is supposed to be the very heart of English verse, not only does not always appear in the exact form of (15), but in fact becomes unbearably tedious if it does so very often! The question, then, is just how we know, when we look at lines like those in (17), that it is iambic pentameter we are dealing with.

(17) a.   Full many a glorious morning have I seen
            Flatter the mountaintops with sovereign eye . . .
                                                        —Shakespeare
      b.   And that one talent which is death to hide
            Lodged with me useless, though my soul more bent . . .
                                                        —Milton
      c.   I do not know much about gods; but I think that the river
            Is a strong brown god .'. .
                                                        —T. S. Eliot

Many attempts have been made to deal with this problem, too, mostly
by listing all the multitude of "exceptions" that are allowed in an iambic
pentameter line (the same thing as listing all the "irregular" verbs of a
language). For instance, it has been customary to state that it was permissible
to invert the first *da DA* and make a *DA da* out of it. (Not very profound,
although it is possible to make it seem scholarly by talking of trochaic feet
instead of *DA da*s.)

As the list of exceptions grew longer and longer, however, it began to
look as though almost anything might constitute an iambic pentameter line,
and as though it would have been simpler to specify such a line as one that
might not extend for more than two-and-a-half inches on the page, or
something of the kind.

Obviously, some generalization was being missed. A clue to the solu-
tion is to be found in the work of Jespersen (in Gross, 1966), where he points
out that it is the *relative* weakness or strength of syllables that is important
to English verse—i.e., the strengths of syllables in comparison with one
another. Jespersen says "Verse rhythm is based on the same alternation
between stronger and weaker syllables as that found in natural everyday
speech."

Morris Halle and Samuel Jay Keyser, following Jespersen's lead, have
now proposed a system to characterize iambic pentameter which has not only
proved entirely adequate but has been extended (by Joseph Beaver) to cover
other English meters as well. This system is based upon the new concept of
the *stress maximum*.

The stress maximum is very new, but not difficult to understand. Like
the tree structures of transformational syntax, it is at the same time clear to
the understanding and satisfying to the intuitions. It is defined as follows:

> (ii) **A stress maximum is a syllable which has an unstressed syllable flanking it
> on either side.**

This means, of course, that neither the first nor the last syllable of a line
could ever constitute a stress maximum, since they have a syllable on only
one side rather than both.

To this definition Keyser and Halle add the following two rules (here somewhat simplified):

> (iii) **An iambic pentameter line consists basically of ten slots which can be filled.**
>
> (iv) **A stress maximum may occupy only *even-numbered* slots, but not all such slots have to be filled.**

To make all this clear, let's look at a few examples. The following line is an ordinary iambic pentameter line chosen from those in (16), and fits the formula of (15) perfectly. The positions within the line are filled by numbered syllables, and those which constitute stress maxima have been outlined.

(18) I saw the ships sail in on Christmas Day.

I	saw	the	ships	sail	in	on	Christ-	mas	Day
1	2	3	4	5	6	7	8	9	10

If you read the line aloud to yourself, you will notice that each of the outlined syllables is more strongly stressed than either of the syllables which flanks it on the right or on the left. This line contains four stress maxima, which means that every possible position for a stress maximum is filled. Now consider the following example:

(19) Look at the ships sail in on Christmas Day.

Look	at	the	ships	sail	in	on	Christ-	mas	Day
1	2	3	4	5	6	7	8	9	10

In this line it is true that the first word, 'look', is more strongly stressed than the word 'at' which follows it. Remember, however, that to constitute a stress maximum a syllable must have a weaker-stressed syllable on *both* sides. Therefore, this line contains only three stress maxima.

In English verse there are time when two syllables may count as one metric syllable. The rules for this are based upon English phonology and are rather complicated, but we can take up one example here. When two syllables are separated only by a *nasal* consonant, they may count as a single metric syllable, as in (20):

(20) I sat in a tree and watched the day go by.

I	sat	in a	tree	and	watched	the	day	go	by.
1	2	3	4	5	6	7	8	9	10

The two syllables of 'in a' are made up of two vowels separated by a single nasal consonant and therefore can fill a single metric position. The line has four stress maxima.

All of the examples above have been very heavily filled. Many English pentameter verse lines have only two stress maxima, and even only one, per ten positions. Obviously the more stress maxima there are in a line the more insistent the rhythm will be, but a succession of lines with four stress maxima very quickly becomes doggerel rather than verse. An important part of the pleasure we get from poetry is in its unexpectedness, its difference, and there is simply nothing unexpected about dozens of uninterrupted repetitions of da-DA-da-DA-da-DA-da-DA-da-DA.

The application of the stress maximum theory to English metrics has had very exciting results. It is now possible to explain why a line is felt by all of us to be iambic pentameter, even when it varies markedly from the old formula based upon the totally non-English concepts of metric feet.

Joseph Beaver has pointed out how this theory can be extended to other English metric patterns. For example, a tetrameter line has eight slots to be filled, a trimeter line has six, and so on. In a trochaic line (the opposite of iambic), the stress maxima would only be allowed to occur in the *odd*, rather than the even, positions, as in example (21):

(21)   Mary, Mary, quite contrary . . .

Ma-	ry	Ma-	ry	quite	con-	tra-	ry
1	2	3	4	5	6	7	8

This line contains three stress maxima, the highest number possible for a tetrameter line. The rhythm is therefore very strongly felt. Most nursery rhymes, jump-rope rhymes, game rhymes, and so on are written with the full utilization of all possible stress maxima. Such rhymes appeal very strongly to children, and are usually easy to remember—which may well be why the pattern is so overwhelmingly popular with the writers of commercials for radio and television.

The theory of stress maxima is one of the most important break-throughs in English stylistics, and is no more than an extension of the principles of alternating stress that are already an essential part of the phonology of ordinary English discourse, as Jespersen pointed out.

Further Applications

Given the concepts that have been developed in this chapter, what are we able to say about the possibilities for their further use?

One of the most important applications of these ideas is to the characterization of literary style. Style is something we all feel, whether we are able to
talk about it or write about it or not. If we read a great deal of the work of
some particular writer, there comes a time when we can pick up a story and
know, without first looking at the credit line, that it is his work. We develop
for the style of particular poets and prose writers the same feeling of recognition that we have for the voices of people we talk to frequently. Even if we
cannot identify one story as by Hemingway and another as by Dickens, we
would never, never make the mistake of identifying the two as being by the
same writer.

This feeling, this recognition of the writer's voice, is what lies behind
the art of literary criticism. When a critic talks about the work of a particular writer, he attempts to explain this, to so characterize the style of the
writer that we can understand and know his work.

There have been as many styles of literary criticism as there have been
styles in the work they criticize. Some of it approaches metaphysics, as in the
"she writes and one hears the roar of the open sea and is sucked into the
vortex of a powerful imagery that carries all before it" school. Some of
it has been statistical, as we said earlier in the chapter—the "does Tennyson
use more *w*'s than Browning?" approach—and we have seen where that leads.
Some of it, a great deal of it, is brilliant, of course.

But if I, discussing Hemingway, talk of his "masculine" style, what do
I mean? Is there any way of knowing whether what I mean by "masculine"
matches in any way your concept, as reader, of "masculine" writing?
Words like *powerful, overwhelming, limpid, fresh, piercing,* all the litany of
English adjectives, have meanings that may not be the same from person to
person. It is here that linguistics may be of significant use.

First of all, the linguist can examine the work of a given writer to see
how and to what extent he employs the *nonliterary* transformations of
English which are not obligatory. If Writer X is very fond of using the
Passive, but Writer Y almost never uses it, then we have a specific fact about
the difference between the two styles. If a writer uses the various deletion
transformations a great deal, the linguist can point this out; something is then
being said about the writer's style that is subject to empirical verification
and that has to mean the same thing for all speakers of English.

At this point it is necessary to avoid a possible source of confusion, by
the way. The natural tendency is to say, "Why is it any better to know how
many *Passives* a writer uses than it is to know how many *w*'s he uses?" The
two seem at first to be parallel.

But this is a mistaken impression. When a writer uses the various
members of the inventory of grammatical transformations, he effects actual
changes, or refrains from making such changes, in the deep structures. Let's

say he begins with the following tree:

(22)

From this single underlying structure it is possible for all of the following sentences to be derived:[1]

(23) a. *John kissed Mary.*

b. *Mary was kissed by John.*

c. *It was John that kissed Mary.*

d. *It was Mary that was kissed by John.*

e. *What John did was kiss Mary.*

When a writer chooses one of these alternatives rather than another it shows nothing at all if it happens only once or twice. But when a consistent preference for one type of surface structure over the others can be shown, then this constitutes a definite characteristic of his style.

The writer is not in quite the same situation in the choice of letters. The letters that make up English words are not his to choose among, they are already given. It is almost impossible for a writer not to use many, many *e*'s, because *e* is by far the most frequent letter in the English language.

What the writer *can* do, particularly in poetry, but also in prose, is show a definite preference for particular *patterns* of sounds by choosing sets of words that contain them. This is what lies behind assonance and alliteration, for example. But the number of instances of a specific letter is far more likely to be the result of the simple facts of spelling dictated by the vocabulary the text requires than a matter of deliberate choice.

Once a writer's patterns of preference for nonliterary transformations have been noted, a linguist can move to his use of the optional literary transformations and search for the same sort of patterns. Finally, the linguist can say something like, "We know of Writer X that he consistently uses transformations A, B, D, E, and S, and that he avoids transformations

---

[1] This statement is not *strictly* true, since all the sentences of (23) are not entirely synonymous. But the inaccuracy here is not important to our discussion, and can be disregarded.

P and Q like the plague." This is very different from stating that his style is "masculine." If enough transformational inventories of this type could be put together and compared, we might even begin to see comparative patterns that would enable us to understand what we mean when we see the style of Hemingway as "masculine" and the style of someone else as less so.

In poetry, of course, the linguist can note the poet's use of stress maxima. Does he show a marked preference for using all possible positions? Does he show a very low incidence of fully utilized lines? Does he have a consistent pattern of alternation, a line with only one stress maximum, then a line with three, then a line with one?

It should be possible to describe not only the styles of various individual writers, but also those amorphous things known as "schools" of writing. This is shown, for example, in the following quotation from Donald C. Freeman (1970, p. 448):

> The shift in metrical style during the sixteenth century from the stiffly formal pentameters of Gascoigne and Grimald to the more flexible verse of Marlowe and Kyd can be characterized . . . as a shift in the metrical ideal from a line with four actualized stress maxima to a line with three.

There is no reason why the use of certain transformations, or certain patterns of stress maxima, should not be as subject to fashion as the decline and fall of such poetisms as *o'er* and *ope*.

Finally, there is the possibility of looking for literary universals. This seems a bit presumptuous at the moment, since we have only the embryonic beginnings of an understanding of the literary structure of our own language.

However, certain things are already known about universal stylistics even at this early stage. First, there is no human society that is *without* a literary language. Second, there is no language which lacks rhythmic devices for its literature, although their forms vary radically from one language to another. Just as every language has a means of indicating negation, although the words and patterns used may be very unlike, so does every language have a way of indicating rhythmic pattern, even though the surface realizations are not the same.

We know something about the recognition conventions of other languages. We know, for instance, that literature cannot be recognized by its status as printed material on a page in a culture that has no written form for its language. In such cultures there will be an oral literature, the most common characteristic of which is likely to be a very high frequency of repetition. (This repetition allows the listener a chance to consider the material at leisure in a manner analogous to that which print offers the reader.) It may be that the literary language is reserved for use on special occasions, or for use by specific persons, such as priests or shamans. In some cultures the literary language itself may be radically different from that of daily discourse, not only in its syntax but in its phonology as well. Thus the

Navajo have a large corpus of religious songs and chants which has systematic differences from the phonology of ordinary Navajo; for example, a Navajo word that in daily speech contains a nasal vowel will almost always be found in songs and chants with an oral vowel plus a nasal consonant.

The literary transformation of *Overlap Deletion* is certainly a device specific to English literary language, particularly English poetry. However, it is interesting to note that this same transformation is also very common in a language as widely removed from English as Japanese, where it is in fact much less constrained than it is in English. I have seen an example of *Overlap Deletion* in a children's poem written in Navajo by a contemporary Navajo poet. There is no reason in principle why this transformation should not turn out to be a universal process of literary language, but much more research would be needed before such a claim could be made.

As linguists work with literary texts, applying to them the principles of linguistic theory, we will learn more and more about literary language. We are just at the beginning, and some of our unsolved problems are monumental. For example, no one has yet come up with a satisfactory definition of a poem, although we all feel that we know one when we see one. Again, no one knows precisely how to characterize the rhythms of free verse, or the rhythms of prose, although we all know that they exist. But the theory of linguistics does give us some scientific tools with which to tackle such problems and a way of setting out the answers so that they are clear to everyone, not just to critics and linguists. This is a definite advance and should make rapid progress possible.

SUGGESTED READINGS FOR CHAPTER SEVEN

TRADITIONAL AND TRANSITIONAL STYLISTICS

CHATMAN, SEYMOUR. "Robert Frost's 'Mowing': An Inquiry into Prosodic Structure." *Kenyon Review* 18 (1956): 421–51.

An interesting and comprehensible article.

GROSS, HARVEY, ed. *The Structure of Verse.* New York: Fawcett World Library, 1966.

This is a good general collection of articles from traditional stylistics. Not difficult.

HERZOG, G. "Some Linguistic Aspects of American Indian Poetry." *Word* 2 (1946): 82.

GONZALEZ, RAFAEL J. "Symbol and Metaphor in Náhuatl Poetry." *Etc.* 25 (1968): 4.

Two brief articles dealing with stylistic analysis of non-Indo-European poetry.

LEVIN, SAMUEL. *Linguistic Structures in Poetry.* The Hague: Mouton, 1962.

This is a transitional book between traditional stylistics and transformational stylistics.

SEBEOK, THOMAS A., ed. *Style in Language*. Cambridge: M.I.T. Press, 1964.

This book is a large and comprehensive collection of articles on all areas of stylistics, with commentaries on the articles and fine bibliographies. Especially recommended is "Linguistics and Poetics" by Roman Jakobson, pp. 350–77.

GENERATIVE TRANSFORMATIONAL STYLISTICS

FREEMAN, DONALD C, ed. *Linguistics and Literary Style*. New York: Holt, Rinehart and Winston, Inc., 1970.

This is the first collection of articles on stylistics with a primarily transformational orientation. Particularly recommended are the following articles (with the warning that the Bierwisch selection is extremely technical): "Poetics and Linguistics," by Manfred Bierwisch, pp. 96–115; "Stylistics and Generative Grammar," by James Peter Thorne, pp. 182–96; "Chaucer and the Study of Prosody," by Morris Halle and Samuel Jay Keyser, pp. 366–426; and "A Grammar of Prosody," by Joseph C. Beaver, pp. 427–47.

GRINDER, JOHN T., and SUZETTE HADEN ELGIN. *A Guide to Transformational Grammar*. New York: Holt, Rinehart and Winston, Inc., 1973. Chapter 12.

An extremely simple introduction to transformational stylistics. Intended for the beginner.

JACOBS, RODERICK A., and PETER S. ROSENBAUM. *Transformations, Style, and Meaning*. Waltham, Mass.: Xerox College Publishing, 1971.

This brief paperback, already cited in the Bibliography for Chapter Two, is the simplest possible discussion of transformations and style. Highly recommended.

VIII

Applied Linguistics

Applied linguistics is simply the application of the principles and theory of linguistics to other areas of knowledge. This definition includes, among other things, work with computers, the programming of texts, speech and hearing therapy, and mathematical linguistics. In this chapter, however, applied linguistics will be discussed only in terms of its use in teaching, which is the area of its widest and most general application.

Teaching the Linguistic Minority Child

The primary example of the practical value of applied linguistics is in teaching children of linguistic minorities, in particular Negro, Chicano, and American Indian children.

For the middle-class white child elementary school is a place much like home. The language spoken is the same. The world pictured in the textbooks *is* home, where a comfortable white house sits in the middle of a neat green lawn, and each family has its Dick and Jane and Spot and Puff and Daddy and Mother. The image the child has of himself is the image that the teacher has of him and expects him to have.

The minority child's situation is radically different. For the Chicano child, and often for the American Indian child, the language of instruction in the elementary school is a foreign language. The black child already speaks English when he begins school, but his English is not the standard dialect that his teacher uses. It is a very different dialect called Nonstandard Negro English (NNE).[1]

These minority children are expected to learn their entire curriculum, including reading, from instruction in Standard American English (SAE). The world pictured in their textbooks is not the world of the ghetto or the barrio or the reservation. From the very beginning the minority child must struggle under a set of handicaps that would destroy an educated adult. (Imagine yourself required to compete on an equal basis at a French university, with French as the only language of instruction and English looked down upon as an unsatisfactory and inadequate substitute for "correct" speech!) The total effect of these handicaps is clear for all to see—examine any set of statistics on the school dropout rate, on unemployment, and on annual family income.

These children suffer not just the long-term effects, but shockingly immediate ones. For example, Philip D. Ortego, in his article, "The Education of Mexican-Americans," points out the following:

> Spanish-speaking Mexican American children have been relegated to classes for the retarded simply because many teachers equate linguistic disadvantage with intellectual ability. In California alone, Mexican-Americans account for more than 40 percent of the so-called mentally retarded.

When the San Francisco, California, school system recently retested in Spanish all the children in classes for mentally retarded who had Spanish last names, they were horrified to find that almost fifty percent of these children were of normal or better than normal intelligence (San Francisco *Chronicle*, January 24, 1970).

No one denies that the situation described above is scandalous. No one denies, either, that the political and economic facts of life in the United States require that these minority children learn to use SAE. But there is no reason why they cannot be helped to do so without in the process destroying their confidence in their own linguistic heritage.

The question is, what can the teacher do? Facing a classroom of forty children or more, as is true for many teachers today, what can a teacher do to change the situation for these children?

---

[1] The word *nonstandard* is not a pejorative term. There are many varieties of nonstandard English, among them the dialects of such areas as Appalachia, northern New England, the deep South, and this writer's native Ozarks.

The very first step lies in a change in the attitude of the teacher himself, a recognition on his part that *there is nothing wrong with the speech of these children.* The children are not too lazy to use English "properly," nor too unintelligent, nor too stubborn. Their speech is simply different.

Consider an example from the speech of the black ghetto child. He has to deal with a mystifying spelling system that contains not only such curiosities as *cough* and *bough* and *through*, but where the word he knows and pronounces /tɛs/ is spelled t-e-s-t, his word /nɛks/ is spelled n-e-x-t, and so on. For him the percentage of words that seem to have little connection between their spelling and their pronunciation is far greater than for the middle-class white child.[2] Every attempt he makes to come to terms with reading reinforces his feeling that the language he speaks is somehow inferior to "real" English.

Phonologists have analyzed the sounds of NNE in order to find and describe its systematic phonological regularities. The problem with *tes'* and *nex'* is the result of the following phonological rule of NNE:

(i) When a word ends in two non-nasal consonants, and the second consonant is either /t/ or /d/, that second consonant is dropped.

The linguistically informed teacher who is aware of this rule can explain to the child that NNE is a dialect of English with the same linguistic status (except in terms of prestige) as any other dialect, and that dialects differ in the presence or absence of particular rules. He can explain to the child that just as the speaker who does not pronounce the *g* in *sign* is following a phonological rule—*not* making a mistake—so is the NNE child following a rule, rather than making a mistake, when he simplifies these final consonant clusters.

Such an explanation will make it clear to the child that his language is only different, not wrong, and that the difference is one that can be predicted and systematically dealt with. When he comes across the word *best* in his textbooks, he will not be mystified by the fact that it ends with the letter *t*.

Similarly, the teacher who is aware of the systematic phonological differences between SAE and NNE will know what kinds of difficulties in reading and understanding to expect, and will not make the mistake of underrating the child when they occur.

For the Chicano child, whose own language has a near-perfect correspondence between spelling and sound, the problems of reading English are

---

[2] The black child will have a comparable difficulty in understanding what he hears because of the high incidence of homonyms in NNE that are not homonymous in SAE. For example, the distinction between final /θ/ and final /f/ does not exist in NNE. Therefore the NNE-speaking child will have trouble hearing the difference between such words as *death* and *deaf*.

a source of despair. In addition, he is going to have trouble understanding what he hears. Let's consider a specific example.

Mexican Spanish has a phoneme /ch/ but no phoneme /sh/. English has many minimal pairs based on the /ch-sh/ distinction. Thus the Chicano child is going to have a hard time distinguishing between *ship* and *chip*, between *shoe* and *chew*.

The teacher who knows of this difficulty and can anticipate it can take specific steps to deal with it. First, he can describe these two sounds to the child in articulatory terms and have the child pronounce them while paying scrupulous attention to what his tongue is doing. The difference between /ch/ and /sh/, in terms a child can understand, is that for /ch/ the tongue tip touches the ridge behind the upper teeth, while for /sh/ it remains firmly against the bottom teeth.

Next the teacher can have the child practice with minimal pairs for these two sounds, listening very carefully and paying attention to what is happening in the mouth. For example, the Chicano child might be asked to repeat the following sentences:

(1) a. *I hurt my shin. I hurt my chin.*

  b. *This is my share. This is my chair.*

  c. *I can't spell 'shoe'. I can't spell 'chew'.*

  d. *'Sheep' is a five-letter word. 'Cheap' is a five-letter word.*

By hearing these forms in close contact, one after the other, and observing the articulation, the child can learn to hear the difference. Hearing only one member of the pair in isolation, no matter how many times, will not help. The teacher should also have the child work with sentences that use both members of the pair, as in the following:

(2) a. *This sheep is cheap.*

  b. *A shoe is not to chew.*

  c. *My shin bumped my chin.*

  d. *I will share my chair.*

In Navajo the distinction between English /p/ and /b/ does not exist, so that the Navajo sound, to the English ear, is often not quite one or the other but something in between. Thus the Navajo child can be expected to have difficulty with English /p-b/ minimal pairs, as the Chicano child has difficulty with /sh-ch/ ones. The following sets of sentences will be helpful to the Navajo child:

(3) a. *I sat on a pin. I sat on a bin.*
     b. *Buy only one pail. Buy only one bale.*
     c. *I can spell 'peril'. I can spell 'barrel'.*
     d. *'Push' is a four-letter word. 'Bush' is a four-letter word.*

(4) a. *Don't push me into that bush.*
     b. *I'm in peril in this barrel.*
     c. *A pin would be hard to find in a bin.*
     d. *Take that pail and bail!*

The teacher can explain the voiced-voiceless distinction to the Navajo child by having him place his fingertips against his Adam's apple and say first *zzzzzz* and then *sssssss*. The vibration the child feels against his fingers when he says a prolonged /z/ is voicing. (Using /p/ and /b/ as voicing examples will not work, because the child will feel the vibration of the vowel sound that has to follow the stop if it is to be pronounced at all, and this vibration will occur with both sounds.)

   It should be the responsibility of every teacher of children whose native speech constitutes a learning handicap (a) to discover exactly where the phonological differences lie, as in the examples given above; (b) to explain them to the child in terms that will not make him feel that he is linguistically inferior; (c) to remain aware of them as a teacher in order to anticipate problems and head them off; and (d) to prepare materials for dealing with these differences in a systematic fashion. One of the best ways to begin such a task is to examine an articulatory chart for the sounds of the child's language side by side with a chart for the sounds of English. Numerous sources for such materials can be located by writing to the Center for Applied Linguistics, 1717 Massachusetts Avenue N.W., Washington, D.C. 20036.

   When two languages are compared in this fashion, the process is called *contrastive analysis*. This method can also be applied to syntactic comparison of pairs of dialects or languages. Consider first an example from NNE. The following sentences are examples of what is called the "progressive" construction of SAE:

(5) a. *She is leaving.*
     b. *He is singing madrigals.*
     c. *I wonder why she is working so hard.*

Notice that in all these sentences we can see the operation of a rule which says, informally, something like "insert the appropriate form of the verb *to be* after the subject, and add *-ing* to the main verb." However, let's look at the progressive sentences from NNE which parallel those of (5):

(6) a. *She leaving.*

b. *He singing madrigals.*

c. *I wonder why she working so hard.*

It is easy to see that one major difference between these two sets of sentences is that in NNE the rule is only "add *-ing* to the main verb." Compare also the following:

(7) SAE $\begin{cases} \textit{They are large.} \\ \textit{They're large.} \end{cases}$

NNE $\begin{cases} \textit{They're large.} \\ \textit{They large.} \end{cases}$

(8) SAE $\begin{cases} \textit{That's what they are.} \\ \textit{*That's what they're.} \end{cases}$

NNE $\begin{cases} \textit{That's what they are.} \\ \textit{*That's what they.} \end{cases}$

Examples (7) and (8) show that wherever SAE can use the mechanism of contraction (*they are → they're*), NNE can use deletion (*they are, they're → they*). On the other hand, where SAE cannot contract the pronoun and the verb *to be*, NNE cannot delete.

A second syntactic difference between these two dialects of English is in the third-person singular form of the English verb. Consider the following:

(9) a. *Rebecca works.*

b. *Michael sings.*

c. *Hermione gargles.*

It is clear here that SAE has a rule, "add the suffix *-s* to the verb form to indicate the third-person singular of regular verbs." However, although it is obvious *what* SAE is doing, it is not so obvious *why*. What functions does this suffix serve? Look at the following examples:

(10) a. **Works.*

b. **Sings.*

c. **Gargles.*

As these examples clearly show, no third-person singular verb form may be used unless it is accompanied by a third-person singular subject *NP*. An element like this *-s*, which is not really necessary at all, is called a *redundant* element. This is further demonstrated in SAE by the fact that none of the modal verbs (*can*, *will*, *may*, etc.) require the use of the third-person suffix. NNE has simply gone one step farther and eliminated the redundant suffix everywhere, so that the NNE parallels to (9) are the following:

(11) a. *Rebecca work.*

     b. *Michael sing.*

     c. *Hermione gargle.*

It is not the case, therefore, that a speaker of NNE is "dropping" this *-s* in speech; in his dialect the suffix has never been added at all, and is not there to be dropped.

The Navajo-speaking child will have difficulty with the English noun plurals, because only a few Navajo words have a separate plural form. He can be expected to produce ungrammatical sentences like the following:

(12) a. **I have only two sweater.*

     b. **I see a lot of book on the table.*

It should be pointed out to him that his language treats the number problem for most nouns as English treats the noun *sheep*, but that the English language usually requires a surface marking for the plural of a noun.

There is much dispute at the moment on how to introduce the children of linguistic minorities to SAE. Some authorities feel that the child should learn in his native language or dialect for the first few years of school, and then be introduced gradually to SAE. Others would provide instruction in both languages, with the child hearing the same material first in his own speech, and then again in SAE, until gradually SAE can be used alone. Most point out that even when the child is fluent in SAE, if his native language is not a dialect of English, his proficiency in that language should be maintained by the school. (The illogic of spending enormous sums to teach English-speaking children Spanish while allowing Spanish-speaking children to forget their native tongue enters into this last proposal.)

These proposals, and others, have appeared in professional journals in the past few years, and have led to some degree of misunderstanding among the minority groups they are designed to help. The following quotation from a recent issue of the NAACP periodical *The Crisis* exemplifies this mis-understanding:

> What our children need, and other disadvantaged American children as well—Indian, Spanish-speaking, Asian, Appalachian, and immigrant Caucasians—is training in basic English, which today is as near an inter-national language as any in the world. To attempt to lock them into a provincial patois is to limit their opportunities in the world at large.

Linguists certainly do not advocate any such "locking in" for these children. The strategy of applied linguistics in this situation is not to prevent minority children from learning to effectively use the prestige dialect of English in the United States today. Instead, it is to allow the linguistic minority child to begin learning the basic skills of literacy without the added handicap of instruction in a foreign language; and to allow the child to become proficient in the prestige dialect of English without destroying his pride and confidence in himself and his own native linguistic heritage.

Teaching Foreign Languages

The principles of contrastive analysis have been widely used in foreign language teaching for a number of years, and textbooks using contrastive techniques are available for the more popular foreign languages, as well as for classes in English as a foreign language.

At the phonological level the teacher proceeds as with the linguistic minority children. That is, he determines where the phonological differences lie and demonstrates them to his students. A very important principle here is *interference*.

Interference occurs at the points where the patterns of the speaker's native language have misleading similarities to patterns of the foreign language. For example, the fact that the orthography of Spanish uses the letter *b* between vowels, where it is pronounced as a fricative rather than a stop, will cause the English speaker to use the English *b* in pronouncing words like *trabajar* and *lobo*. Similarly, the difference between the alveolar English /t/, /d/, and /n/, and their dental French counterparts, is so slight that the English pattern interferes in the acquisition of the French pattern.

The examples so far have illustrated techniques for dealing with phono-logical differences in language. Now let's consider an example of a technique for teaching syntactic differences developed by Sauer and reported in Selinker

(1971). Consider the following:

(13)

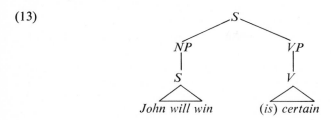

From this particular deep structure the English speaker has the option of generating any of the following sentences:

(14) a. *That John will win is certain.*

b. *It is certain that John will win.*

c. *John is certain to win.*

Spanish has an equivalent deep structure, as shown in (15):

(15)

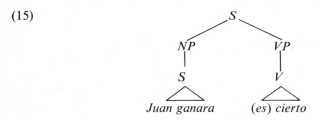

However, the possible surface structures for Spanish are not the same as English. The pattern is shown in the following:

(16) a. *That John will win is certain.*
Que Juan ganara es cierto.

b. *It is certain that John will win.*
Es cierto que Juan ganara.

c. *John is certain to win.*
*Juan es cierto ganar.

Because of the close correspondence between the English pattern and the Spanish one, the English speaker is almost sure to produce the ungrammatical Spanish sentence in (16c).

The teacher should determine the areas of syntactic interference, such as this one, and warn the students against them by a clear demonstration of the systematic patterning involved, as in (16).

The material in this chapter has presented only a brief sketch of the possibilities available to the teacher through applied linguistics. Much of the usefulness of linguistics for the teacher lies not just in the techniques described in this chapter, but in the basic principles linguistic theory has developed for language learning, of whatever kind.

For example, the teacher can now be aware that there is no language which is "harder" than any other. There are languages for which certain skills are initially easier than for others. For example, reading is going to be slower for the student who must master an entirely different alphabet, as in the study of Russian, than for the student of Spanish, who not only has the same alphabet to read with as in English, but an alphabet that matches the Spanish sound system very closely. But the initial discrepancies in learning speed among languages will level out during the course of an ordinary instruction sequence (say a three-year course at the high school level, or two years at the college level), so that the final degree of proficiency obtained with Russian will be no less than with any other so-called easier language.

The realization that there is system underlying the apparent surface disorder in human languages is of great help to the teacher. He can apply this principle to such problems as spelling irregularities, "irregular" verbs, and many other areas.

It would be possible to continue with examples of the relevancy of linguistics for teaching and fill up several volumes. Experiments and pilot projects that apply the theory of linguistics, both traditional and generative, to all sorts of learning situations are being initiated everywhere today; and accounts of these experiments can be found in numerous professional journals. The application of linguistics to the study of reading, to freshman composition courses and to classes in literary analysis is showing great promise.

Because of the potential value of such studies for teachers, the bibliography for this chapter is somewhat different than the previous ones. Instead of a careful choice of sources intended primarily for nonlinguists, this bibliography is intended to offer the widest possible variety of materials, among which the reader may choose.

SELECTED READINGS FOR CHAPTER EIGHT

ALATIS, JAMES E., ed. *Contrastive Linguistics and Its Pedagogical Implications.* Washington, D.C.: Georgetown University Press, 1968.

————. *Linguistics and the Teaching of Standard English to Speakers of Other Languages or Dialects.* Washington, D.C.: Georgetown University Press, 1969.

————. *Bilingualism and Language Contact: Anthropological, Linguistic, Psychological, and Sociological Aspects.* Washington, D.C.: Georgetown University Press, 1970.

ALLEN, HAROLD B. *Readings in Applied English Linguistics.* New York: Appleton-Century-Crofts, Inc., 1958.

ANDERSSON, THEODORE. "Bilingual Education: The American Experience." *Modern Language Journal* 55 (1971): 427–440.

HORN, THOMAS D., ed. *Reading for the Disadvantaged: Problems of Linguistically Different Learners.* New York: Harcourt Brace Jovanovich, 1972.

HOUSTON, SUSAN H. "A Sociolinguistic Consideration of the Black English of Children in Northern Florida." *Language* 45 (1969): 599–607.

HUGHES, JOHN P. *Linguistics and Language Teaching.* New York: Random House, Inc., 1968.

LAMB, POSE. *Linguistics in Proper Perspective.* Columbus, Ohio: Charles E. Merrill Publishing Company, 1967.

LEFEVRE, CARL A. *Linguistics and the Teaching of Reading.* New York: McGraw-Hill Book Company, 1964.

MALSTROM, JEAN, and JANICE LEE. *Teaching English Linguistically: Principles and Practices for High School.* New York: Appleton-Century-Crofts, Inc., 1971.

O'BRIEN, RICHARD J., S. J., ed. *Languages and Linguistics: Working Papers* (Nos. 1, 2, and 3). Washington, D.C.: Georgetown University Press, 1970 and 1971.

ORNSTEIN, JACOB. "Sociolinguistic Research on Language Diversity in the American Southwest and Its Educational Implications." *Modern Language Journal* 4 (1971): 223–29.

POLITZER, ROBERT L. *Teaching French: An Introduction to Applied Linguistics.* Waltham, Mass.: Blaisdell Publishing Company, 1965.

———. *Foreign Language Learning: A Linguistic Introduction.* Englewood Cliffs, N.J: Prentice-Hall, Inc., 1965.

———. *Teaching German: An Introduction to Applied Linguistics.* Waltham, Mass.: Blaisdell Publishing Company, 1968.

———. *Practice-Centered Teacher Training: French.* Vol. 1, No. 2575. Philadelphia: Center for Curriculum Development, 1970.

———. *Practice-Centered Teacher Training: Spanish.* Vol. 1, No. 2576. Philadelphia: Center for Curriculum Development, 1970.

———, and CHARLES N. STAUBACH. *Teaching Spanish: An Introduction to Applied Linguistics.* Waltham, Mass.: Blaisdell Publishing Company, 1965.

ROSENBAUM, PETER S. "On the Role of Linguistics in the Teaching of English." In *Language and Learning*, eds. Janet A. Emig, James T. Fleming, and Helen M. Popp. New York: Harcourt Brace Jovanovich, Inc., 1965.

JOURNALS

Florida Foreign Language Reporter, 1969. Vol. 7, No. 1. *Linguistic-Cultural Differences and American Education.*

Florida Foreign Language Reporter, 1972. Vol. 9, Nos. 1 and 2. (A special supplementary issue devoted entirely to black language and culture.)

(Both of the above available at 801 NE 177th Street, North Miami Beach, Florida 33162.)

Language Learning: A Journal of Applied Linguistics. Ann Arbor, Mich.: English Language Institute, University of Michigan.

Field Linguistics

Throughout this text the discussion of linguistic work has been confined almost entirely to studies done in an academic or semi-academic situation. This emphasis may have left the impression that such studies constitute the only kind of linguistic work. However, one of the most interesting types of study that linguists do does not require an academic situation at all—the linguistic specialty called *field linguistics*, or "field work."

In field linguistics the linguist studies a language and learns about it not from published materials or from a professional language teacher but from direct contact with a native speaker of the language.

In theory there is no reason why a linguist should not study any language whatsoever in this fashion. A linguist who had had no instruction in French might decide to learn it by direct contact with a French speaker, and he would be doing field linguistics. Nor, in theory, does a linguist really have to go "out into the field" to do field work. In fact, much field work today is done in nonfield situations. For example, a linguist at a university may do field linguistics with a native speaker of Cherokee who is a student at that university.

In this chapter, however, the discussion will be restricted to the more traditional type of field linguistics, that which is responsible for the term itself. In this sort of field work the linguist leaves the academic environment and goes directly to the people whose language he wants to study. Ideally, he actually lives among them. If this is not feasible, he will spend as many hours as he possibly can in the field, in direct contact with native speakers in their own environment.

The native speaker who helps the linguist to learn about his language is called an *informant* (not to be confused with "informer"). In the field situation the informant is the expert, and the linguist is the learner. Thus the choice of an informant is of crucial importance. Just as it may be difficult to learn an academic subject from a poor teacher, it is going to be difficult to learn a language in the field from a poor informant. If the linguist has a choice—which will not always be the case—he will make a very careful decision in this regard.

Since the linguist must have the cooperation of the people he is working with, and since it is by no means certain that they will be delighted to have him among them, it often happens that a lot of time in the field must be devoted to winning the trust of these people and gaining their acceptance of the idea of having their language studied and described. The linguist who forgets this essential first step runs a number of risks: he might be given inadequate or deliberately incorrect information; he might be ordered to leave and never come back; he might even be killed with a poisoned spear.

After winning the necessary acceptance and cooperation, the linguist must next find out what the meaningful sounds of the language are; that is, he must establish an inventory of the phonemes of the language. This can be a difficult task, especially if the studied language contains many sounds that are not meaningful in the linguist's native language. For example, compare the list of English phonemes in Table I with the list of Navajo phonemes in Table II. You will see that they are very different.

TABLE I

ENGLISH PHONEMES

Consonants: p, b, t, d, k, g
                       f, v, θ, ð, s, z, h
                       sh, zh, ch, j
                       m, n, ŋ
                       l, r
                       w, y

Vowels: ɨ, ɛ, æ, ə, ʊ, ɔ, a
                       iy, ey, uw, ow

TABLE II

NAVAJO PHONEMES

Consonants: b, t, t', d, dz, dl, k, k', g'
              s, z, h, x, gh, hw
              ts, ts', tl, tł', l, ł
              sh, zh, ch, ch', j
              m, n
              w, y

Vowels: i, ɨ, ɛ, o, a
              į, ɨ̨, ɛ̨, o̧, a̧,
              ai, ao, ei, i, oi

You can see at once that there are many more consonants in Navajo than in English, and some of them very formidable-looking. If you heard them pronounced you would find them equally formidable-sounding. This is not because they are intrinsically more difficult to pronounce than English consonants, but because they are absent from the inventory of English sounds and therefore totally new to the English speaker's vocal organs. For example, English has no sounds like the Navajo phonemes /ł/ and /ł'/.

It may also happen that a sound which occurs in the language being studied is also present in the linguist's native language but is not considered to be meaningful. English, for example, does have the consonantal segment called a *glottal stop* (written /'/ in Table II). To hear a glottal stop, pronounce the phrase 'a apple'; you can only do so by inserting a glottal stop between the word 'a' and the first letter of 'apple'. In some dialects of English, words like *bottle* and *shuttle* are pronounced with a glottal stop between the /t/ and the /l/ sounds. But the glottal stop is not a phoneme of English, and the English speaker is not accustomed to noting its presence or absence.

In Navajo, on the other hand, there are minimal pairs which can be differentiated only in this way. Particularly when the distinction is made at the end of a word, it is difficult for the linguist newly exposed to the language to tell the pair apart. For example, the sequence /baa/ means 'to him', but the sequence /baa'/ is a girl's name.

Some African languages have as phonemes sounds that are called *clicks.* We use clicks in English when we make the sound of disapproval written "Tsk-tsk," when we want a horse to start moving, and when we are imitating the sound of a kiss. But in languages with click phonemes the various kinds of click are exactly as meaningful as the phonemes /p/ and /m/ and /o/ are to the speaker of English.

The linguist attempting to establish a phoneme inventory will look for minimal pairs, one basic strategy for achieving this goal. If he is working with Navajo he will notice that there is a word pronounced /tin/, meaning 'ice', and a word /kin/, meaning 'store'. From this and similar pairs he will be able to determine that Navajo has a phoneme /t/ and a phoneme /k/.

The linguist may go about this in a number of ways, depending on the communication situation. For instance, if his informant happens to speak English, or if he and the informant share some common language, the linguist can proceed rather directly. He says, "How do you say ——" and the informant provides him with the proper word or words, which he then writes down. If the linguist and the informant have no language in common, they may have to work through an interpreter, which is less satisfactory. Worst of all is the situation where no interpreter is available and the linguist and informant share no language at all. In this case the linguist will resort to whatever communicational strategies he can devise, using gestures, intonation, facial expressions and whatever else seems useful. Perhaps the most typical beginning strategy in such a situation is that of touching an object or pointing to it to elicit the name.

As the linguist hears a word he writes it down on a slip of paper with what he assumes to be its correct meaning, and he collects many of these slips, each with its own word. A major problem, of course, is in determining just what *is* a word—that is, where the word boundaries are. If a field linguist were working with English, and English was still an unwritten language, he might have a great deal of difficulty deciding which of the following was the correct word division:

a norange	a naunt	a nantelope
an orange	an aunt	an antelope

Nor would sequences like 'a napkin' and 'a notebook' be helpful. Only after he had heard many sequences of indefinite article followed by noun would the linguist realize that there might be two words *a* and *an*, one to be used before words beginning with a vowel and the other before words beginning with a consonant. And only after hearing a sequence like 'the orange' could he determine that *orange* in modern English begins with a vowel, and that the *n* sound is not a part of that word.

After establishing an inventory of phonemes, the linguist will attempt to determine what are the *morpheme structure rules* of the language—that is, what combinations of phonemes into morphemes are possible. In Navajo, for example, he will notice that many Navajo words begin with /ts/ but that none end with it. Therefore the sequence /. . . ts#/ is forbidden in Navajo, while the sequence /#ts. . ./ is perfectly all right.

Assume that the linguist has recorded a large number of morphemes of the language, that he knows what phonemes they are composed of, and that he has a basic idea as to the morpheme structure rules. His next step will be to think about the syntax of the language he is studying. He will determine what constitutes a sentence in the language, and what sub-parts constitute its major parts. He will determine in what order constituents must occur to be grammatical. As he reaches a stage of facility with the language that allows him to write down sentences instead of just a word or two at a time, he watches carefully for sentences that seem to form sets, from examination of which he may be able to make generalizations. He will propose sentences to his informant and see if they are accepted or rejected. He will investigate the mechanisms the language has for forming questions, commands, and negatives. He will work constantly with his collected data in an attempt to prepare a set of syntactic rules for the language.

In addition, the field linguist must of course delve into the semantics of the language he is studying. If the semantics differs greatly from his native language it is likely to cause considerable difficulty. Problems may arise even at the stage where he is merely writing down the names of objects. For example, if an English-speaking linguist were to ask a German speaker how to say 'table' in German he would be given the word *Tisch*. Similarly, if he asked a French or Spanish speaker, he would be given a single morpheme which functions as does the word 'table' in English.

In Navajo, however, the equivalent for 'table' is *biká adaní*, and it may be a long time before he learns that the sequence is translated literally 'that upon which eating is done'.

Similarly, if a linguist sets up a sequence like 'Give me the ——' and starts substituting various words in English, French, or German in the blank, he will find that just about any noun will fit and the rest of the sentence will stay the same. But in Navajo he will continually be stopped and told that the sentence is ungrammatical. The problem here is that Navajo has a set of classifying verbs, among which is the verb for 'give', and the form of the verb will vary according to the physical characteristics of the object given. To give someone a sheet of paper, which is flat, will require a different verb form than that needed for giving a basketball, which is round.

Determining the relevant characteristics for assigning a particular noun to its class is not always going to be easy. For example, in Navajo if you talk of cornflakes in a box, you need one verb form; the same cornflakes, dry in a bowl, will require another. If milk is added and the whole thing gets a bit mushy, the verb form changes again; and for cornflakes spilled on the floor you will need still another form. Such semantic hurdles as these can hold a field linguist back for a long time, because they conceal the syntactic generalizations that could otherwise be made.

From the foregoing presentation it might be inferred that the linguist first isolates the phonemes, next he moves on to the problem of what constitutes a word, then he tackles the problems of syntax, and so on, one step after the other. Although all these steps do take place, in actual fact they are usually overlapping. The linguist in field work is continually acquiring material from all areas of the grammar. He gets a phonological fact here, a syntactic fact there, a bit of semantic material at the same time, and he sorts it out as best he can as he goes along. The preceding discussion of methodology, then, should be looked upon as only a broad description of what actually happens.

A question is sometimes raised as to why field work is done, and what relevance it has. Many languages studied by field linguists are rapidly dying out, and there may be no more than a handful of native speakers left. It is not unusual for a linguist to do field work with the last living speaker of a particular language. Certainly no great demand is likely to arise for classes in such languages, particularly when—as is usually true—there exists no written literature in the language. That is, although there are no more living native speakers of Latin, the great Latin written literature provides a clear motivation for learning the language; this situation does not hold true for most languages studied in the field.

One answer to this question lies in the hypothesis of universal grammar. Our current information about what a human language may be like is based on only a tiny sample of the existing languages of the world. Based upon our current limited information, linguists propose universals such as that no language has nasal vowels unless it also has oral vowels, or that no language lacks a mechanism for asking questions. We need many, many more facts about languages before we can really make universal statements with confidence, and we have no way of knowing, before we study a language, what it may have to contribute to the total store of linguistic knowledge.

Another reason why field work is important is that it throws new light on our knowledge of more commonly studied languages. The science of linguistics suffers from the handicap of not being able to see the forest for the trees just as does any other science. A linguist finds it hard to avoid the trap of always looking at the same set of problems from exactly the same point of view.

A linguist who investigates in depth the system for indicating the possessive in an American Indian language, or the passive sentence in an Australian language, will almost always find that this provides him with ideas about the description and analysis of the English possessive and passive that would never otherwise have occurred to him.

Because the results of field linguistics can be of such importance to linguistics as a whole, it is extremely important that they be as complete and as accurate as possible. No one any longer feels comfortable publishing an article on field linguistics that is based on only a few hours of contact with a language, or even a few days. Instead, linguists try to spend significant amounts of time in field work with a language and to work with more than just one or two informants before publishing their results.

This means that field linguistics, if properly done, is going to require great patience and determination from both linguist and informant. The linguist may be anxious to get on with his work with the negative sentence, while the informant prefers to talk about some personal matter. If the linguist insists on sticking to his subject, the result may be an offended informant, obviously a bad situation for further work. Conversely, the informant may find it boring, not to say simple-minded, to sit for an hour giving paradigms of verbs or plurals of nouns. Field linguistics is not a suitable specialty for anyone who has difficulty in handling interpersonal relationship.

Unfortunately, even the best analysis done in the field by a linguist, with the help of the very finest informant, is never going to be good enough. We will never have satisfactory grammars of previously undescribed languages until they can be prepared by trained linguists who are also native speakers of those languages. The proper person to write a grammar of Cherokee or Samoan is a Cherokee or Samoan native speaker who is also a linguist, and the lack of such people is one of the tragedies of the current linguistic scene. We can only hope that it is a lack that will be speedily remedied.

SELECTED READINGS FOR CHAPTER NINE

Although a vast number of descriptions of specific field work studies are available, not much has been written on the actual techniques and methods of field linguistics. Three basic sources are listed below; for the many individual reports of field studies the student should consult linguistic and anthropological journals, in particular, IJAL (International Journal of American Linguistics).

BLOCH, BERNARD, and GEORGE L. TRAGER. *Outline of Linguistic Analysis.* Baltimore, Maryland: Linguistic Society of America, 1942.

This is a traditional description of methods in field linguistics.

HALE, KENNETH. "On the Use of Informants in Field-work." *The Canadian Journal of Linguistics* 10 (1965): 108–19.

This is an excellent non-technical article on the linguist-informant relationship and the methods and principles underlying that relationship. Highly recommended.

SAMARIN, WILLIAM J. *Field Linguistics: A Guide to Linguistic Field Work.* New York: Holt, Rinehart and Winston, Inc., 1967.

This book is the only really complete text on field linguistics available. It is clearly and interestingly written and can be used by the beginning student with ease. Highly recommended.

Bibliography

ALATIS, JAMES E., ed. *Contrastive Linguistics and Its Pedagogical Implications.* Washington, D.C.: Georgetown University Press, 1968.

————. *Linguistics and the Teaching of Standard English to Speakers of Other Languages or Dialects.* Washington, D.C.: Georgetown University Press, 1969.

————. *Bilingualism and Language Contact: Anthropological, Linguistic, Psychological, and Sociological Aspects.* Washington, D.C.: Georgetown University Press, 1970.

ALLEN, HAROLD B. *Readings in Applied English Linguistics.* New York: Appleton-Century-Crofts, Inc., 1958.

ANDERSSON, THEODORE. "Bilingual Education: The American Experience." *Modern Language Journal* 55 (1971): 427–40.

BEVER, THOMAS G. "The Cognitive Basis for Linguistic Structure." In *Cognition and the Development of Language.* New York: John Wiley & Sons, 1970.

BLOCH, BERNARD. "A Set of Postulates for Phonemic Analysis." *Language* 24 (1948): 3–46.

BLOOMFIELD, LEONARD. *Language.* New York: Holt, Rinehart and Winston, Inc., 1933.

BODMER, FREDERICK. *The Loom of Language*. New York: W. W. Norton and Company, Inc., 1944.

BRÉAL, MICHEL. *Semantics: Studies in the Science of Meaning*. New York: Dover Publications, Inc., 1964.

BROOK, G. L. *A History of the English Language*. New York: W. W. Norton and Company, Inc., 1958.

Brown, R. and A. Gilman. "The Pronouns of Solidarity and Power" In *Style in Language*, ed. T. Sebeok. Cambridge: M.I.T. Press, 1960.

CHADWICK, JOHN. *The Decipherment of Linear B*. Cambridge: Cambridge University Press, 1958.

CHATMAN, SEYMOUR. "Robert Frost's 'Mowing': An Inquiry into Prosodic Structure." *Kenyon Review* 18 (1956): 421–51.

CHOMSKY, NOAM. *Syntactic Structures*. The Hague: Mouton, 1957.

———. *Language and Mind*. New York: Harcourt Brace Jovanovich, Inc., 1968.

CHURCH, JOSEPH. *Language and the Discovery of Reality*. New York: Vintage Books, 1966.

DEESE, JAMES. *Psycholinguistics*. Boston: Allyn & Bacon, Inc., 1970.

DENES, PETER B., and ELLIOT N. PINSON. *The Speech Chain*. New York: Bell Telephone Laboratories, Inc., 1963.

ELGIN, SUZETTE HADEN. "The Crossover Constraint and Ozark English." In *Syntax and Semantics*, ed. John Kimball. New York: Academic Press, 1973.

FISHMAN, JOSHUA A., ed. *Readings in the Sociology of Language*. The Hague: Mouton, 1968.

FODOR, J., and T. BEVER. "The Psychological Reality of Linguistic Segments." *Journal of Verbal Learning and Verbal Behavior* 4 (1956): 414–20.

FREEMAN, DONALD C., ed. *Linguistics and Literary Style*. New York: Holt, Rinehart and Winston, Inc., 1970.

GARDNER, R. ALLEN, and BEATRICE T. GARDNER. "Teaching Sign Language to a Chimpanzee." *Science* 165 (1969): 664–72.

GARRETT, M., T. BEVER, and J. FODOR. "The Active Use of Grammar in Speech Perception." *Perception and Psychophysics* 1 (1966): 30–32.

GLEASON, HENRY A. *An Introduction to Descriptive Linguistics*. New York: Holt, Rinehart and Winston, Inc., 1961.

GONZALEZ, RAFAEL J. "Symbol and Metaphor in Náhuatl Poetry." *Etc.* 25 (1968): 4.

GRINDER, JOHN T., and SUZETTE HADEN ELGIN. *A Guide to Transformational Grammar*. New York: Holt, Rinehart and Winston, Inc., 1973.

GROSS, HARVEY, ed. *The Structure of Verse*. New York: Fawcett World Library, 1966.

HALLE, MORRIS. "Phonology in a Generative Grammar." In *The Structure of Language*, eds. Jerry A. Fodor and Jerrold J. Katz. Englewood Cliffs, N.J.: Prentice-Hall, Inc., 1964.

HARMS, ROBERT. *Introduction to Phonological Theory*. Englewood Cliffs, N.J.: Prentice-Hall, Inc., 1968.

HARRIS, ZELLIG. "Co-occurrence and Transformation in Linguistic Structure." In *The Structure of Language*, eds. Jerry A. Fodor and Jerrold J. Katz. Englewood Cliffs, N.J.: Prentice-Hall, Inc., 1964.

HERZOG, G. "Some Linguistic Aspects of American Indian Poetry." *Word* 2 (1946): 82.

HOCKETT, CHARLES F. *A Course in Modern Linguistics*. New York: The Macmillan Company, 1958.

――――. "A System of Descriptive Phonology." *Language* 18 (1942): 3–21.

HORN, THOMAS D., ed. *Reading for the Disadvantaged: Problems of Linguistically Different Learners*. New York: Harcourt Brace Jovanovich, Inc., 1972.

HOUSTON, SUSAN H. "A Sociolinguistic Consideration of the Black English of Children in Northern Florida." *Language* 45 (1969): 599–607.

HUGHES, JOHN P. *Linguistics and Language Teaching*. New York: Random House, Inc., 1968.

JACOBS, RODERICK A., and PETER S. ROSENBAUM. *Transformations, Style, and Meaning*. Waltham, Mass.: Xerox College Publishing, 1971.

JAKOBSON, ROMAN. "Aphasia as a Linguistic Problem." In *On Expressive Language*, ed. H. Werner. Worcester, Mass.: Clark University Press, 1965.

KATZ, JERROLD J., and JERRY A. FODOR. "The Structure of a Semantic Theory." In *The Structure of Language*, eds. Jerry A. Fodor and Jerrold J. Katz. Englewood Cliffs, N.J.: Prentice-Hall, Inc., 1964.

KAY, MARTIN. "From Semantics to Syntax." In *Progress in Linguistics*, eds. Manfred Bierwisch and Karl Erich Heidolph. The Hague: Mouton, 1970.

KEILER, ALLAN R., ed. *A Reader in Historical and Comparative Linguistics*. New York: Holt, Rinehart and Winston, Inc., 1972.

KIPARSKY, PAUL. "Linguistic Universals and Linguistic Change." In *Universals in Linguistic Theory*, eds. E. Bach and R. T. Harms. New York: Holt, Rinehart and Winston, Inc., 1968.

LADEFOGED, PETER. *Elements of Acoustic Phonetics*. Chicago: University of Chicago Press, 1962.

LAMB, POSE. *Linguistics in Proper Perspective*. Columbus, Ohio: Charles E. Merrill Publishing Company, 1967.

LeFEVRE, CARL A. *Linguistics and the Teaching of Reading*. New York: McGraw-Hill Book Company, 1964.

LENNEBERG, E. *The Biological Foundations of Language*. New York: John Wiley and Sons, Inc., 1967.

――――. "On Explaining Language." *Science* 165 (1969): 664–72.

LEVIN, SAMUEL. *Linguistic Structures in Poetry*. The Hague: Mouton, 1962.

LOTZ, JOHN. "Linguistics: Symbols Make Man." In *Frontiers of Knowledge*, ed. L. White, Jr. New York: Harper and Brothers, 1956.

LYONS, JOHN. *Introduction to Theoretical Linguistics*. Cambridge: Cambridge University Press, 1969.

McDAVID, RAVEN. "Postvocalic -r in South Carolina: A Social Analysis." *American Speech* 23 (1948): 194–203.

MALSTROM, JOAN, and JANICE LEE. *Teaching English Linguistically: Principles and Practices for High School.* New York: Appleton-Century-Crofts, 1971.

O'BRIEN, RICHARD J., S. J., ed. *Languages and Linguistics: Working Papers* (Nos. 1, 2, and 3). Washington, D.C.: Georgetown University Press, 1970 and 1971.

ORNSTEIN, JACOB. "Sociolinguistic Research on Language Diversity in the American Southwest and Its Educational Implications." *Modern Language Journal* 4 (1971): 223–229.

ORTEGO, PHILIP D. "The Education of Mexican Americans." In *The Chicanos: Mexican American Voices*, eds. Ed Ludwig and James Santibañez. Baltimore: Penguin Books, Inc., 1971.

OSTWALD, PETER F. "Acoustic Methods in Psychiatry." *Scientific American* March 1965, pp. 82–92.

POLITZER, ROBERT L. *Teaching French: An Introduction to Applied Linguistics.* Waltham, Mass.: Blaisdell Publishing Company, 1965.

———. *Foreign Language Learning: A Linguistic Introduction.* Englewood Cliffs, N.J.: Prentice-Hall, Inc., 1965.

———. *Teaching German: An Introduction to Applied Linguistics.* Waltham, Mass.: Blaisdell Publishing Company, 1968.

———. *Practice-Centered Teacher Training: French.* Vol. 1, No. 2575. Philadelphia; Center for Curriculum Development, 1970.

———. *Practice-Centered Teacher Training: Spanish.* Vol. 2, No. 2576. Philadelphia; Center for Curriculum Development, 1970.

———, and CHARLES N. STAUBACH. *Teaching Spanish: An Introduction to Applied Linguistics.* Waltham, Mass.: Blaisdell Publishing Company, 1965.

ROSENBAUM, PETER S. "On the Role of Linguistics in the Teaching of English". In *Language and Learning*, eds. Janet A. Emig, James T. Fleming, and Helen M. Popp. New York: Harcourt Brace Jovanovich, Inc., 1965.

SAPIR, EDWARD. *Language.* New York: Harcourt Brace Jovanovich, 1921 and 1949.

SCHANE, SANFORD. *Generative Phonology.* Englewood Cliffs. N.J.: Prentice-Hall, Inc., 1973.

SEBEOK, THOMAS A., ed. *Style in Language.* Cambridge: M.I.T. Press, 1964.

———. "Communication in Animals and in Man: Three Reviews." In *Readings in the Sociology of Language*, ed. Joshua A. Fishman. The Hague: Mouton, 1968).

SELINKER, LARRY. "A Brief Reappraisal of Contrastive Linguistics." In *Working Papers in Linguistics*, University of Hawaii, April 1971, p. 3.

STOKOE, WILLIAM C., Jr. *A Dictionary of American Sign Language on Linguistic Principles.* Washington, D.C.: Gallaudet College Press, 1965.

TRAUGOTT, ELIZABETH CLOSS. "Diachronic Syntax and Generative Grammar." *Language* 41 (1965): 402–15.

ULLMANN, STEPHEN. "Semantic Universals." In *Universals of Language*, ed. Joseph H. Greenberg. Cambridge: M.I.T. Press, 1966.

WATERMAN, JOHN T. *Perspectives in Linguistics.* Chicago: The University of Chicago Press, 1963.

Index